D0788882

DATE DUE

GAYLORD			PRINTED IN U.S.A.

MODERN WORLD NATIONS

AFGHANISTAN	IRAQ
ARGENTINA	IRELAND
AUSTRALIA	ISRAEL
AUSTRIA	ITALY
BAHRAIN	JAMAICA
BERMUDA	JAPAN
BOLIVIA	KAZAKHSTAN
BOSNIA AND HERZEGOVINA	KENYA
BRAZIL	KUWAIT
CANADA	MEXICO
CHILE	THE NETHERLANDS
CHINA	NEW ZEALAND
COSTA RICA	NIGERIA
CROATIA	NORTH KOREA
CUBA	NORWAY
EGYPT	PAKISTAN
ENGLAND	PERU
ETHIOPIA	RUSSIA
FRANCE	SAUDI ARABIA
REPUBLIC OF GEORGIA	SCOTLAND
GERMANY	SOUTH AFRICA
GHANA	SOUTH KOREA
GUATEMALA	TAIWAN
ICELAND	TURKEY
INDIA	UKRAINE
IRAN	UZBEKISTAN

Jamaica

Janet H. Gritzner
South Dakota State University

Series Consulting Editor
Charles F. Gritzner
South Dakota State University

CHELSEA HOUSE
PUBLISHERS
A Haights Cross Communications Company

Philadelphia

Frontispiece: Flag of Jamaica

Cover: The Archives Office is one of the buildings in Spanish Town Square, Jamaica.

CHELSEA HOUSE PUBLISHERS

VP, NEW PRODUCT DEVELOPMENT Sally Cheney
DIRECTOR OF PRODUCTION Kim Shinners
CREATIVE MANAGER Takeshi Takahashi
MANUFACTURING MANAGER Diann Grasse

Staff for JAMAICA

EXECUTIVE EDITOR Lee Marcott
PRODUCTION EDITOR Megan Emery
PICTURE RESEARCH 21st Century Publishing and Communications, Inc.
SERIES DESIGNER Takeshi Takahashi
COVER DESIGNER Keith Trego
LAYOUT 21st Century Publishing and Communications, Inc.

A Haights Cross Communications ⬥ Company

http://www.chelseahouse.com

First Printing

1 3 5 7 9 8 6 4 2

Library of Congress Cataloging-in-Publication Data

Gritzner, Janet H.
  Jamaica/by Janet H. Gritzner.
    v. cm.—(Modern world nations)
Includes index.
Contents: Introducing Jamaica—Natural environment—History—People and culture—
Administration and government—Economy—Living in Jamaica today—Jamaica looks to
the future.
  ISBN 0-7910-7913-9
  1. Jamaica—Juvenile literature. [1. Jamaica.] I. Title. II. Series.
F1868.2.G75 2004
972.92—dc22
                                                                    2003028099

Table of Contents

Jamaica

1

Introducing Jamaica

On a blustery January day, would you like to be on a tropical island? Come to Jamaica, a country of sun-drenched beaches, warm tropical breezes, and a rich cultural heritage. Jamaica is an island nation and a close neighbor of the United States. It is a masterpiece of tropical splendor and extraordinary vistas. The natural landscape is filled with the multicolored hues of exotic plants and flowers and is subdued by the various green shades of dense rain forests, woodland and grass-covered meadows, and misty valleys. Countless cascading waterfalls tumble down from the mountainous interior, feeding the rivers, which spread out like hundreds of fingers across the island. White sand beaches rim the north and west sides of Jamaica, and the scenic Blue Mountains dominate the eastern side of the country. Jamaica is a great place for a vacation, and the island paradise attracts thousands of visitors each year.

White sand beaches rim the north and west sides of the island and bring thousands of tourists to Jamaica each year.

Jamaica is located in the southwest Caribbean Sea, only about 550 miles (885 kilometers) south of Miami, Florida. It is the third-largest island in the Greater Antilles, the island chain that also includes Cuba, Hispaniola, and Puerto Rico. Because it is so close to the United States, you or someone you know may have been to

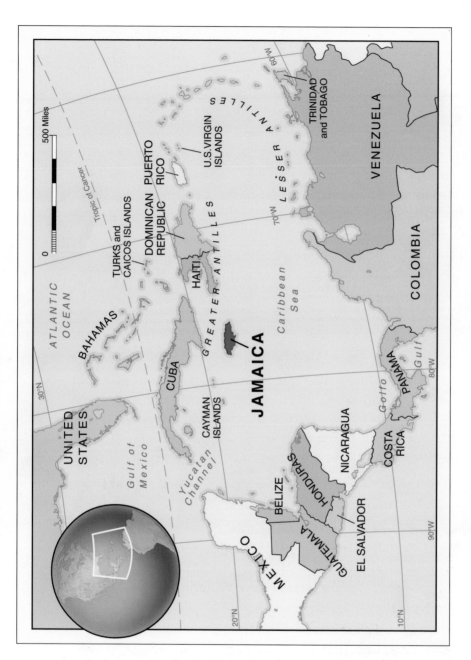

Jamaica is located in the Caribbean Sea about 550 miles (885 kilometers) south of Miami, Florida. It is the third-largest island in the island chain that includes Cuba, Hispaniola, and Puerto Rico.

Jamaica. What did you notice, or what did people tell you about the country? Did you know that the national motto of the country is "Out of many, one people" and that it speaks to the ethnic diversity of Jamaica? The majority of Jamaicans are of African descent, but there are well established, although relatively small, East Indian, Chinese, Arab, and European communities as well. Jamaican culture draws from all these groups. Popular culture, however, is heavily influenced by Jamaicans' African heritage, and formal behavior is unmistakably British in style.

The islands of the Caribbean form stepping stones that stretch in an arc from the western end of Venezuela in South America to the peninsula of Florida in the United States. The Caribbean Islands are divided into two groups: the larger, east-west situated Greater Antilles, which form the northern part of the arc, and the smaller, north-south aligned Lesser Antilles, which form the eastern part. The Greater Antilles include the four large islands of Cuba, Hispaniola (made up of the countries of Haiti and the Dominican Republic), Jamaica, and Puerto Rico. The Lesser Antilles are made of numerous smaller islands, including groupings known as the Windward and Leeward islands, as well as Barbados, Trinidad and Tobago, and the French Islands of Guadeloupe and Martinique.

"West Indies" is the name given to island nations in the Caribbean that have English as the official language and are members of the British Commonwealth. Jamaica is the largest of the English-speaking West Indian islands. It has an area of 4,244 square miles (10,991 square kilometers), making it slightly smaller than the state of Connecticut. Of that, 4,182 square miles (10,832 square kilometers) is land area and a relatively small area of 62 square miles (160 square kilometers) is water. The island measures 146 miles (243 kilometers) from east to west and is 51 miles (80 kilometers) at its point of greatest north-south width. The distance from Kingston, the capital, located on the south coast, to Annotto Bay, the nearest point on the north coast, is a mere 22 miles (36 kilometers).

Jamaica's nearest neighbors are Cuba, 90 miles (150 kilometers) to the north, and Haiti, 100 miles (160 kilometers) to the east. Centrally situated in the Caribbean region, it lies on direct sea routes from the United States and Great Britain to the Panama Canal.

Jamaica is divided into three counties and 14 parishes. Each parish has a main town, in which the government offices for the parish are located. Kingston, founded in 1692 after a violent earthquake devastated the city of Port Royal, became the country's capital in 1872. Previous British capitals were Port Royal and Spanish Town.

Spanish Town, named for its Spanish settlers, is one of the oldest continuously occupied cities in the Western Hemisphere and is a major population center in Jamaica today. Kingston is the heart of island life. It is a modern, bustling, sprawling city that never seems to sleep. The city is situated on a wide plain with the sea to the south and the Blue Mountains as its backdrop to the north. Kingston and it neighboring parishes are highly urbanized and draw their population from all over the island. As long ago as the 1970s, the question was asked, "How many people can this part of the island provide living space for?" The answer was far fewer than the number of people who want to come to the capital to live and work.

Jamaica is a country of contrasts. It has a multitude of problems such as urban sprawl, poverty, crime and violence, a depressed economy, and high foreign debt. Yet it is country of incredible scenic beauty, with many natural resources and a rich cultural life. Through the pages of this book, you will travel through Jamaica's varied and beautiful natural landscapes, study the country through time, and learn about the island nation's people, culture, government, and economy. You will get a glimpse of what life in Jamaica is like today, and you will gaze into a crystal ball to project the country's future.

2

Natural Environment

J amaica has a rich and varied natural environment. The island's land features range from low-lying coastal plains to the Blue Mountain crests reaching nearly 7,500 feet (2,286 meters) in elevation. Part of the island is a lush tropical paradise, and some areas are dry much of the year making them almost desertlike in appearance and character. The island is rich in a variety of resources, including bauxite (the ore from which aluminum is made), and suffers from occasional natural hazards, including devastating hurricanes.

ORIGIN OF A CARIBBEAN ISLAND

With a few exceptions, the islands of the West Indies are actually the summits of a range of submarine volcanic mountains. Over millions of years, this range has undergone episodes of uplift followed by subsidence (sinking or settling to the bottom), leaving all but the highest peaks covered by water. Jamaica's Blue Mountain

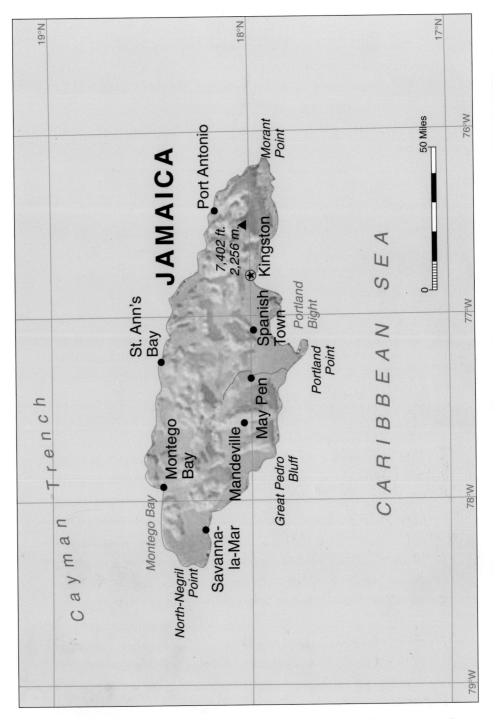

Jamaica's land features range from low-lying coastal plains to the Blue Mountain crests that reach nearly 7,500 feet (2,286 meters) in elevation.

range is the oldest and highest of the mountains on the island. During the period of most active uplifting and folding, the Blue Mountains pushed up to over 7,000 feet (2,134 meters). Blue Mountain Peak, the highest point in Jamaica and one of the highest peaks in the entire Caribbean region, towers 7,402 feet (2,256 meters) above the island's surrounding terrain. Four other peaks rise above 6,000 feet (1,830 meters). They are Sugar Loaf, the country's second highest point, with an elevation of 7,055 feet (2,150 meters), and High, Mossman's, and Sir John peaks. Only the highest mountains of the Dominican Republic (over 10,000 feet, or 3,048 meters) and Haiti (over 9,000 feet, or 2,743 meters) stand taller than the Blue Mountains of Jamaica.

On a clear day, the range is visible from nearly all points on the island. Seen from a distance, it appears blue in color, as is the case with the Blue Ridge Mountains in the central Appalachians. In both locations, atmospheric moisture creates a haze that gives the ranges a blue cast.

During periods of submergence under the sea, thick limestone deposits were formed. Limestone is a sedimentary rock that is created from the remains of sea creatures, including coral. Yellow limestone was formed first and was overlaid by white limestone layers. More than half of Jamaica's surface is covered by white limestone overlying yellow limestone. Over time, dissolving of the white limestone led to the development of depressions (solution basins) and extensive cave networks. Some depressions have an almost circular shape and have filled-in areas of bright red earth (bauxite). Bauxite is the source of aluminum metal. Sizes of individual deposits vary from small pockets to large basins of more than 309 acres (125 hectares) and in thickness from several feet to more than 98 feet (30 meters). Bauxite mining is the second-largest industry in Jamaica.

Waters of the rivers flowing through the white or yellow limestone or red earth material take on the color of the land:

Some are nearly white and others are yellow to orange. Several thousand years ago, Phoenician voyagers from the eastern Mediterranean region sailed to some undocumented distant land. When they returned, they told of a land where rivers flowed with waters resembling "milk and honey." Could they have reached Jamaica 2,000 years before Columbus? Some historical geographers think so.

PHYSICAL REGIONS

Jamaica can be divided into three physical regions: an eastern mountainous region, a central and western plateau, and coastal lowlands. Two-thirds of the country is covered with soft, porous limestone. Nearly half of Jamaica is more than 1,000 feet (304 meters) above sea level, with elevations rising gradually from west to east and culminating in the Blue Mountains.

Eastern Mountain Region

In the east, the Blue and John Crow mountains dominate the physical landscape. The Blue Mountain range is formed from a central ridge of metamorphic rock (rock hardened under heat and pressure) running in a northwest to southeast direction with many long spurs jutting north and south. The John Crow Mountains, lying to the north and east of the Blue Mountains, are formed from a strongly tilted limestone plateau, which rises to elevations of more than 3,700 feet (1,138 meters). The Rio Grande River separates the two mountain ranges. This mountainous region is picturesque and rugged, and it is here that the famous Blue Mountain coffee is grown.

Central and Western Plateau Region

Sculpted limestone blocks and other karst formations dominate the central and western plateau region. Karst is formed by solution weathering (when limestone rock is chemically dissolved by water) and erosion. The results of this unique kind of rock

The main route into the mountain is the B1, or Blue Mountain Highway. This narrow road is quite difficult to negotiate and landslides sometimes occur during the rainy season.

decomposition include sinkholes, caves and caverns, disappearing streams, and haystack-shaped hills, all of which are typical features of a karst landscape. High limestone plateaus separated from each other by north- and south-flowing streams and by underground rivers dominate the center of the island. Hector's and Cave rivers are notable examples of rivers whose flow is partially underground. The Mocho, Dry Harbor, May Day, Don Figueroa, and Santa Cruz mountains are all found in the central part of the island. They range in elevation from 1,500 to 2,200 feet (457 to 610 meters), with several peaks. To the west of the central plateaus lies the rugged terrain of the Cockpit Country, a truly dramatic example of karst topography.

The Cockpit Country

The Cockpit Country is identified by its varying landscape of gently rolling soil-covered plains to a rough jumble of deep depressions, isolated towers, and pointed hills. It is the result of karst (solution) weathering and erosion of white and yellow limestone groups, which vary considerably in purity, hardness, and depth. The Cockpit Country represents an especially well-developed topography of bowl-shaped depressions, called cockpits for their resemblance to cockfighting pits, and cone-shaped peaks. It is recognized globally as the type locality for this pattern of aboveground karst. Until well into the twentieth century, this area, because of its rugged terrain, was very isolated. Many escaped slaves sought refuge in the Cockpit Country, where they came to be known as "Maroons."

Coastal Lowlands Region

Coastal lowlands are formed from stream deposits of rivers flowing both to the north and south coasts of the island. The plains are narrow on the north coast but elsewhere extend far inland to the limestone foothills. Major lowlands exist in the southern half of the island, where they are often associated with coastal mangrove (a type of tree or shrub) swamps. This land-building process is continuing along the south coast, with a large fan delta rising at the mouth of the Yallahs River and an extensive submarine shelf building up seaward.

Many of the Jamaica's 120 rivers are dry for most of the year, but they fill rapidly during periods of heavy rainfall, causing extensive local flooding. Three large rivers are the Rio Grande, which collects much of the drainage of the northeast slopes; the Yallahs River, which drains to the southeast; and the Black River, which originates in the Cockpit Country and flows to the southwest coast. The Black River is the largest river and the only navigable stream on the island. The Black River Lower Morass, located near the mouth of the river, is recognized as an internationally significant wetland. This largely freshwater swamp covers 14,085 acres (5,700 hectares) and contains a mix of peat lands, mangrove forests, and limestone islands.

SOILS

The most important influences on soil development in Jamaica are the parent materials (rocks and stream deposits), climate, and vegetation. There are four major soil groups: upland plateau soils, alluvial soils (soils containing material deposited by running water), highland soils, and a catchall category of "others." Upland plateau soils, terra rossa (red limestone soil) and rendzina (black marl; marl is a deposit with a large amount of calcium carbonate), account for 64 percent of the island's soils. Rendzina is a clay soil formed over yellow limestone and marl. Moderately deep and relatively fertile, they have good agricultural potential. Terra rossa, formed over white limestone, are poorer soils that are low in nitrogen, phosphorus, and potassium. Although they contain substantial organic matter, they also have high concentrations of iron and aluminum, giving a distinctive brownish-red "brick" color to the soils. Alluvial soils are loams, sands, and gravel deposited by streams and make up about 14 percent of the country's soil. They are the most fertile and productive soils on the island. Because they are stream-deposited, alluvial soils are located on the coastal plains, inland basins, and valleys. Highland soils, formed in mountainous terrain, account for another 11 percent of Jamaica's soil and are concentrated in the Blue Mountains. The highland soils tend to be porous and susceptible to

The Black River is the largest river and only navigable stream on Jamaica. River rafting is a unique attraction, but many people also go by boat to the wetlands area, which is renowned for its plant and animal life.

leaching (the removal of nutrients) and erosion under conditions of high rainfall.

WEATHER AND CLIMATE

Jamaica has a tropical climate that is somewhat moderated by the cooler waters of the surrounding sea and highlands of the interior. Average daily temperatures along the coast and lowlands average about 79°F (26°C) and range only about

4°F (about 1 to 2°C), from a seasonal low of 78°F (26°C) in February to a high of 82°F (28°C) in August. Temperature extremes also do not have a great range. Rarely do they climb into the 90s (low 30s Centrigrade) or drop into the 50s (low teens Centrigrade). Humidity is high, however, averaging more than 75 percent throughout most of the year and often reaching 100 percent. The moist air makes temperatures feel "hot and muggy." Similar conditions exist during the summer months in the Southeastern United States. Jamaica's mountainous interior has somewhat lower temperatures and humidity. In general, the temperature decreases about 3.5°F (1°C) with each 1,000-foot (300-meter) increase in elevation. Nighttime cooling is also more pronounced at higher elevations.

Mean annual rainfall over the island is about 78 inches (1,980 millimeters). The main dry season lasts from December to April, and peaks in rainfall occur in May and October. Much of the rainfall results from the moisture-laden northeast trade winds, which, when forced upward over the mountain ranges, deposit most of their precipitation on the northern slopes. The southern half of the island experiences a rainshadow effect, receiving notably lower amounts of rainfall. A similar condition exists in Washington, Oregon, and northern California. The windward (western) slopes of the Cascade Mountains are extremely moist, but east of the mountains, desert conditions prevail. Rainfall on the northeastern slopes of the Blue Mountains ranges from 100 to about 200 inches (3,000 to 5,000 millimeters) a year. On the rainshadow-influenced south central coastal plains of St. Catherine and Clarendon parishes, less than 60 inches (1,500 millimeters) of rain falls each year. In the tropical climate, however, the evaporation rate is high, so much less moisture is actually available for plants. Some locations have an almost desertlike vegetation cover. The much drier conditions on the southern half of the island have important consequences for community water supplies and agriculture.

Jamaica's wet north, drier south, and varied mountainous pattern of precipitation are reflected in the types of natural vegetation occurring on the island. Dense tropical forest occurs under natural conditions in areas of high rainfall areas, and mixed forest, grasslands, and scrub (stunted trees and shrubs) grow in areas of low rainfall and high evaporation.

NATURAL HAZARDS

Jamaica's greatest natural hazards are hurricanes, flooding, earthquakes, and landslides. The island is regularly the victim of tropical storms and hurricanes. Strong winds and high amounts of intense rainfall, which often contribute to severe flooding and massive landslides, characterize these often violent weather events. The hurricane season lasts from July to November. Nearly 70 hurricanes (sustained winds above 74 miles per hour, or 119 kilometers per hour) and tropical storms (39 to 73 miles per hour, or 63 to 118 kilometers per hour) have struck the island between 1886 and 2003.

Hurricane Gilbert was one of the strongest Atlantic hurricanes ever recorded. The deadly storm roared into the Caribbean Sea and approached Jamaica on September 12, 1988, with sustained winds averaging 75 miles per hour (121 kilometers per hour) and gusts up to 127 miles per hour (204 kilometers per hour). Barometric pressure continued to drop and winds intensified as the storm struck Jamaica. Atmospheric pressure ultimately dropped to 888 millibars, which is the second-lowest pressure ever recorded for an Atlantic hurricane. Screaming winds reached 180 miles per hour (290 kilometers per hour), making it one of the most intense Atlantic hurricanes in recorded history. Gilbert devastated Jamaica as it raked the entire length of the island, killing an estimated 50 people and affecting another 810,000. Nearly everyone on the island suffered some damage and loss.

Jamaica lies near the northern edge of the Caribbean Plate—a huge mass of Earth's crust—that is thought to be moving in an east-northeasterly direction with respect to the North American Plate. As a result of this movement, earthquakes and the accompanying landslides are common in Jamaica and pose a real threat to life and property. The country experiences up to 200 detectable earthquakes a year. Records of earthquakes in Jamaica date back to the sixteenth century.

Port Royal Earthquake

The Port Royal earthquake of June 7, 1692, is perhaps the most famous of the early earthquakes. Just before noon, a violent quake struck the densely populated city of Port Royal (the city was located on a sand spit, a piece of land jutting into the sea, just southeast of present-day Kingston). In less than five minutes, three shocks, each of greater intensity, caused the sea to recede and then rush back with tremendous force. A wave six feet (1.82 meters) high swept the bay, and much of the city sank into the sea. Earthquake tremors and resulting land subsidence (settling or sinking) destroyed 90 percent of the city's buildings and most of the ships in the harbor. Between 1,500 and 2,000 of the city's 6,500 people were killed by the earthquake and the accompanying tidal wave.

Other major earthquakes occurred in Jamaica in 1712, 1722, 1744, 1812, 1907, and 1957. The earthquake of January 14, 1907, was particularly destructive, leveling both Kingston and nearby rebuilt Port Royal. Kingston, then a town of 46,000, was reduced to rubble in a matter of minutes, and fires raged for up to four days after the quake. More than 800 people died on that day. After the devastating quake, Kingston was rebuilt. The city now is home to nearly one-third of the island's population, which clearly is at risk from future earthquakes.

PLANT AND ANIMAL LIFE

Natural vegetative patterns have been strongly modified by agriculture, mining, and forest industries. Had humans not intervened, the northern coast and the central plateau region would have remained thickly forested. The drier southern plains would have supported a natural vegetation cover of grass, sedges, cacti, acacia scrubland, and scattered tropical trees such as the lignum vitae and cottonwood.

Human Activities and Vegetation

For centuries, Jamaicans have cut mahogany and other cabinet woods in the mountain forests, leaving little of the natural woodland still standing. Only an estimated 6 percent of virgin forest remains. Mountains that at one time were entirely covered by tropical forest now show signs of accelerating deforestation and soil erosion. Hurricanes, floods, landslides, and especially the mining of bauxite, building of tourist resorts, and encroaching coffee plantations, are blamed for the loss of woodlands. Yet pockets of relatively undisturbed vegetation, now in protected reserves, do remain on the island.

Jamaica has more than 128 protected sites that encompass well more than 386 square miles (1,000 square kilometers) of land area. Blue Mountains/John Crow Mountains National Park was established in 1990 to provide stricter protection for government land and designated forest reserves. The park covers 313 square miles (809 square kilometers) and houses the watershed for the city of Kingston and all communities on the eastern third of Jamaica. Much of the Cockpit Country, an area of 166 square miles (430 kilometers), has forest reserve status. Other important forest and wildlife preserves are the Negril Environmental Protection Area, Portland Bight Protected Area, Montego Bay Marine Park, and the Black River Lower Morass.

Lush, diverse vegetation characterizes Jamaican plant life in the less developed areas. The island boasts an extraordinary number of endemic (native) plant species. Among the world's islands, Jamaica ranks fifth in the diversity of native plants and animal species. More native ferns (100) are found in Jamaica than on any other Caribbean Island. Of the 3,000 flowering plant species in Jamaica, more than 750 are native to the island and not found anywhere else. Because of its climate, the island is especially hospitable to orchids. There are 260 species of orchids, 60 of which are native to the island. They vary from very tiny to a diameter of about four inches. Native trees include mahogany, cedar, ironwood, logwood, sandalwood, rosewood, ebony, coconut palm, palmetto palm, and pimento. The blossom of blue lignum vitae is Jamaica's national flower. Introduced ornamental trees such as the red poinciana, colorful bougainvillea, yellow poui, and hibiscus are common throughout the settled areas of the island, providing a year-round spectacle of color.

Animal Life

Jamaica, like a number of the other Caribbean islands, has a highly diversified bird population. The island has more than 200 bird species, 28 of which are native. Common birds include parrots, cuckoos, hummingbirds, and at sea, pelicans. The national bird is the swallowtail hummingbird, also called the "doctor bird." Reptiles are numerous, with 27 different species native to the island. Human activity has severely reduced natural habitats, and as a result, most of the small native mammals have disappeared or are endangered. There are no large mammals. The only native land mammal is the endangered Jamaican hutia, or coney, a large brown rodent resembling a guinea pig. The Blue Mountain/John Crow Mountains National Park is a last refuge for conies as well as home to the giant swallowtail butterfly. The mongoose, introduced from India in the nineteenth century to control snakes in the sugar fields, is seen in the wild. It is considered a pest, because it eliminated the snakes and turned to eating chickens.

Though small in size, Jamaica boasts an incredible variety of terrain, vegetation, and animal life that is unique and special. Jamaicans see ecotourism as a growing industry, through which people can come to the island and enjoy the abundance of nature, which is protected, preserved, and enhanced.

3

History

Jamaica has a remarkable and dramatic history, one of merging peoples and cultures. The island's inhabitants enjoy a culture that is a blend of traditions from various groups that have come to the island over time. They include the native Taino Indians, the English colonizers, and Africans who were introduced to the Caribbean to perform slave labor on the European-owned plantations. There are also people of East Indian and Chinese descent. In recent years, many Canadians and Americans have made Jamaica their home.

TAINO INDIANS

Jamaica's original inhabitants were Taino Indians, an Arawak people originally from the nearby Guyana coastal area of South America. Taino settled the island around 650 A.D., indicating that they had the ability to island-hop using boats of some type. The

An archaeologist with the Jamaica National Heritage works at a site in Inverness where Taino artifacts were discovered in June 2000. The site is rich in artifacts from these original inhabitants of Jamaica.

name "Jamaica" comes from the Arawak word *Xaymaca*, which means "land of wood and water." The Taino were a farming people who grew cassava, sweet potatoes, maize (corn), fruits, vegetables, cotton, and large amounts tobacco. They built villages throughout the island, but most were on the coasts and near rivers to be close to the fishing. Fish was a major part of the Taino diet. The Taino, estimated to number about 100,000, led a relatively peaceful life until the arrival of the Spaniards.

SPANISH RULE

Christopher Columbus landed on the northern coast of the island on May 4, 1494, claiming it for the king and queen of Spain. Fifteen years later, in 1509, the Spanish founded Sevilla Nueva (New Seville) near the present town of St. Ann's Bay on the north coast. Santiago de la Vega (Spanish Town), the Spanish capital city, was established in 1538. For 146 years, Jamaica was a Spanish colony. Within four decades of Spanish rule, the Taino Indians were virtually eradicated. Most died as result of diseases introduced by Europeans against which they had no natural resistance. Others died from hard labor forced on them by their conquerors. No full-blood Taino remain today. As the Taino population declined, the labor they had provided was replaced by African slave labor. Spanish settlers raised cattle and pigs and introduced two things that would profoundly shape the island's future: sugar and slaves.

MAROONS, BUCCANEERS, AND SLAVES

British forces defeated Spanish forces and took control of Jamaica in 1655. On May 10, a body of English sailors and soldiers landed at Passage Fort in Kingston harbor and marched toward Spanish Town. The next day, the Spaniards surrendered. They were allowed a few days to leave the island. Some of them went to Cuba, but others secretly went to the north side of Jamaica.

Slaves released or abandoned by the fleeing Spanish took refuge in the mountains and in the rugged and nearly inaccessible Cockpit Country. There, they established the first "Maroon" communities. Maroon numbers grew with the addition of runaway slaves from British plantations. The name Maroons was taken from the Spanish word *cimarrones,* meaning "unruly, fugitive, and wild." Skirmishes with British troops eventually escalated into two separate Maroon Wars, the second of which led to the deportation of a number of Maroons to Nova Scotia in Canada and eventually to Sierra Leone in West Africa. For

145 years, Maroons fought the British. Peace treaties eventually gave the Maroons self-government and the rights to land they inhabited, and many descendents of original Maroon families still live on the land in Maroon communities.

Slave Trade

Spain formally ceded Jamaica to England in 1670. After the British takeover, the island was turned into a vast sugar cane plantation. With the need for a large labor force accustomed to a hot, humid climate, the British turned to Africa. Several million Africans were brought to the Caribbean region as slaves, hundreds of thousands of them to Jamaica to work the plantations. The Africans were from many tribes: Although the majority were Fante, Ashanti peoples from the Gold Coast (Ghana), there were also Ibo, Edo, and Yoruba from Nigeria and Mandingo from Guinea.

Port Royal and the Buccaneers

Port Royal was Jamaica's commercial center until the devastating earthquake of 1692, when much of the city sank into the sea. Spanish Town became the new capital, and the city of Kingston was founded across the bay. In the late 1600s, Jamaica was a British possession surrounded by Spanish- and Portuguese-held territory. For most of this time, Spain and England were at war. Port Royal was a deep and safely protected harbor and was centrally located along the trade routes between Panama and Spain. Port Royal became the headquarters of buccaneer raids of Spanish vessels carrying gold and silver.

Buccaneers were originally French, Dutch, and English sailors, many of whom had fled their countries to escape the law. The English used the term to refer to the sea rovers or raiders of the Caribbean. Between 1665 and 1671, English buccaneers under the leadership of Sir Henry Morgan sacked 18 Spanish-American cities, 4 towns, and 35 villages and

Nearly 300 years ago Port Royal was called the most wicked place on earth. It was Jamaica's commercial center until the earthquake of 1692 that left much of the area under water. These guns at Fort Charles helped to make Port Royal a safely protected harbor.

captured ships too numerous to count. Much of the plunder obtained on the raids flowed through Port Royal. The town earned the reputation as being one of the wickedest in the world, as well one of the richest for its size.

Sir Henry Morgan, Buccaneer

Henry Morgan was probably the most successful and famous pirate of his time. He had a reputation for harsh brutality yet was respected as a skilled businessman and brave sailor. He acquired the reputation for keeping a cool head under pressure and for the ability to take advantage of favorable circumstances. Morgan was arrested in 1672 for fighting after peace had been arranged between Spain and England and was sent to England to answer to piracy charges. Indeed his immense stolen wealth and tales of his skills and bravery earned a pardon from King Charles II. Morgan was treated like a hero: He was knighted and appointed lieutenant governor of Jamaica in 1674, charged with the task of putting an end to piracy!

JAMAICA: THE SUGAR ISLAND

Jamaica reached its peak under British rule in the eighteenth century, when it was the world's largest producer of sugar and a strategically important military base. Other island activities included cattle raising, coffee growing, logging, and the cultivation of crops such as pimento (allspice), ginger, and arrowroot. The island was virtually self-governing, and its planters (along with those of Barbados) controlled an influential bloc of votes in the English parliament. It was a violent time that suffered numerous slave revolts, pirate raids, Maroon attacks, epidemics, and devastating hurricanes. The region continued to be a war zone fought over by several European powers: England, France, Spain, and the Netherlands. All the while, Jamaica was prospering on sugar.

Great Houses of Jamaica

Many of the "Great Houses"—huge plantation homes—of Jamaica were built during the sugar boom. Most are now in ruins, but several of the surviving houses have been opened to tourists because of their architectural charm and often-colorful histories. One of the best preserved is Prospect Great House. It also is still used as a residence. Rose Hall

Rose Hall Great House is one of Jamaica's major tourist attractions. It was built as a large plantation home in 1760 by the Honorable J. Palmer and is still used as a residence today.

Great House is one of Jamaica's major tourist attractions. It was formerly the home of Annie Palmer, the "white witch" of Rose Hall. As the story goes, Annie Mae Patterson was an incredibly beautiful young woman. She was also an expert in voodoo, having learned voodooism from her nursemaid as a child in Haiti. John Palmer was bewitched, and after he married her, he died of a mysterious illness. He was the first of her three husbands, all of whom experienced similar deaths. Their bodies are said to be buried beneath tall palms growing near the beach opposite the Great House.

Plantation Labor

The limiting factor in the sugar economy was labor. Slaves were always in short supply. In 1834, there were about 650 sugar estates, ranging in size from 800 to 3,000 acres (325 to 1,215 hectares), on the island. Only about 100,000 acres (40,469 hectares) were actually planted in cane. Most of estate land was pasture, waste, or provision grounds worked by slaves in their off-hours.

The death rate among the slaves was extremely high. Between 1702 and 1807, more than 400,000 slaves were imported for use in Jamaica, yet when the British slave trade was abolished in 1807, the slave population was only 319,351. Slave rebellions were not uncommon. In 1782, Jack Mansong, better known as Three-Fingered Jack, led a slave rebellion in St. Mary's Parish. Three-Fingered Jack was a fierce and famous bandit who was the subject of many songs, stories, and even a London play. He patrolled the nearby hills and valleys and fought, often single-handedly, a war of terror against the English soldiers and planters. A chivalrous outlaw who never harmed a woman or child, he was finally ambushed and killed by a Maroon bounty hunter who pickled his head and his three-fingered hand in rum and took them to Spanish Town to claim his reward.

The last and largest of the slave revolts in Jamaica was the 1831 Christmas Rebellion. This uprising was inspired by "Daddy" Sam Sharpe, an educated slave and lay preacher who incited passive resistance. The rebellion turned violent, however: As many as 20,000 slaves razed plantations and murdered planters. When the slaves were tricked into laying down arms with a false promise of abolition, 400 of them were hanged and hundreds more were whipped. There was such a wave of revulsion in England that the Jamaican parliament was forced to abolish slavery.

The End of Slavery

Slavery ended on August 28, 1833, and a system of apprenticeship was put in place. This arrangement allowed slaves to become totally free over a period of four to six years. Slaves finally were given full freedom on August 1, 1838. Some former slaves chose to work on the sugar estates, but many did not. The sugar industry suffered a further blow in 1848. At that time, Great Britain adopted a policy of free trade, allowing goods from foreign countries to enter the English market on the same terms as goods from the British colonies. Jamaica was unable to compete with Cuba and other foreign sugar-producing countries.

After emancipation, many of the ex-slaves settled down as small farmers in the mountains, cultivating steep hill slopes far away from the plantations. Others settled on marginal lands on the plains nearby the plantations. These lands were leased or purchased through various land settlement schemes organized and sponsored by Christian groups such as the Baptists. During this period of peasant history, from about 1838 to 1938, there were many struggles and battles over land (and because of their role in assisting with land ownership, there was an increase in the membership of nonconformist churches). The colonial government treated former slaves poorly. In 1865, the deadly Morant Bay Rebellion erupted as a protest against injustices of the court system and lack of services for the poor.

As a result of the Morant Bay Rebellion and the related deaths of national heroes Paul Bogle and George William Gordon, a new era in Jamaica's development began. The British government was compelled to make reforms in education, health care, local government, banking, and infrastructure. In the aftermath of the rebellion, Jamaica's assembly voted away its traditional independence and became a full crown colony of Great Britain.

Throughout this period, sugar production declined. Indentured workers and free laborers from Central Africa,

India, China, and Europe (primarily Germans, Scots, and Portuguese), replaced freed slaves on the plantations. The greatest number of immigrants came from India. Today, settlements of Indian descendents can still be found in the major sugar cane farming belts.

THE NATIONAL MOVEMENT

Roots of a national independence movement took root in the nineteenth-century struggles for land. More specifically, it was inspired by the political ideas of Marcus Mosiah Garvey, another one of Jamaica's proclaimed national heroes. In the 1930s, political life was reborn. Two very different men, Alexander Bustamante and Norman Manley (who happened to be cousins), founded Jamaica's two most enduring political institutions and the labor unions affiliated to them—the Jamaica Labour Party (JLP) and the People's National Party (PNP). Both men have been declared national heroes for their individual and combined efforts in securing political independence from Great Britain. After World War II, Jamaicans migrated to Great Britain and the United States in large numbers seeking better job opportunities. The United States began to replace Great Britain as Jamaica's principal trading partner, and the island's economy became more varied. It included bauxite and alumina processing and tourism, as well as the export of sugar, bananas, and other agricultural products.

AFTER INDEPENDENCE

On August 6, 1962, Jamaica was granted full independence from Great Britain, with Sir Alexander Bustamante as the first prime minister. The first two governments were formed by the JLP. The postwar boom in the economy continued through the 1960s. Between 1972 and 1980, the PNP, the other major political party, held political office and initiated a shift in major economic policies. Michael Manley, son of Norman Manley,

Seen from behind, with his arm around the shoulder of U.S. Vice President Lyndon Johnson, Sir Alexander Bustamante celebrates Jamaica's independence from Great Britain on August 6, 1962. That day ended 300 years of colonial rule of the island.

was prime minister. At this time, the government began to take a leadership role in the process of economic development. The Bauxite Levy of 1974 was enacted to increase Jamaica's share of the income in the bauxite/alumina industry. Under Manley, Jamaica joined the Caribbean Community and Common Market (CARICOM), a framework for cooperation with other English-speaking Caribbean nations.

JLP regained control in 1980, electing Edward Seaga. The government pursued free market polices, leading to the deregulation of the economy, devaluation of the Jamaican dollar, and privatization of many industries. These policies, in moderated form, have continued to the present.

LOOKING AHEAD

At the dawn of the twenty-first century, Jamaica is struggling both politically and economically. It is a young country with little experience in nationhood and relies on the world economy for most of its money. Many of its citizens, who have a well-earned reputation for hard work, are unable to find jobs at home and must leave the island to better themselves, thus Jamaica is sending many of its best people out of the country. These people are vital human resources that the country desperately needs to succeed as a modern nation.

4

People
and Culture

POPULATION TRENDS

Size of population is an important characteristic of any country. It determines the number of houses, schools, and hospitals; the size of the labor force; and the amount of food and water it is likely to need. The total population of Jamaica in July 2003 was an estimated 2.7 million, with an annual growth rate of .61 percent. Growth rate is defined as the average annual percent change of population, which is calculated by subtracting deaths from births and taking into account migrants entering and leaving the country. This growth is consistent with the governmental target for growth of less than .8 percent over the medium term and a projected population size of less than 3.0 million by the year 2020. In 2003, the estimated average number of children born per woman was 2.01, the figure that equates zero population growth (ZPG). Net migration was an estimated loss of 5.78 migrants per 1,000 population in 2003. Managed population growth is a key factor in sustainable development, which also must deal with the problems of poverty, environment degradation, crime, and violence.

MIGRATION

Movement of people within and out of Jamaica has been going on for decades. Out-migration continues to characterize the Jamaican population shift. People leave the country for better employment and educational opportunities elsewhere. It is estimated that in 2002, the country's population declined by 23,160, primarily as a result of out-migration. Jamaican migration to England and, later, to the United States and Canada, began during the post-World War II era and has continued to the present. As a result of many decades of heavy emigration (out-migration), half of all Jamaicans now live outside of Jamaica. Most emigrants went to the eastern United States, or to England, with large concentrations in New York and London. Money sent home helps to support the Jamaican economy. In fact, money sent from family members outside the country amounted to 13.3 percent of Jamaica's GDP in 2001. Growth in remitted money now rivals tourism and commodity exports as an earner of foreign exchange.

DISTRIBUTION OF POPULATION

Although population numbers often distinguish one country from another, it is usually the density of people (the number of people per unit of land) that is more important. In 2003, population density for Jamaica was an estimated 645 persons per square mile (249 persons per square kilometer), which is relatively high for the Caribbean and Latin America (in comparison, the United States has a density of 78 people per square mile, or 30 persons per square kilometer). Among the parishes, Kingston has the highest population density: It has the largest number of people and is the smallest parish. The town scats (parish capitals) are usually the towns with the highest population in the parishes.

In 2003, the following towns, listed in order, are the most populous in the country: Kingston, 590,000; Spanish Town, 133,400; Portmore, 113,400; Montego Bay, 93,500; May Pen, 49,700; Mandeville, 44,000; Half-Way Tree, 19,900; Savanna-la-Mar, 18,800; Port Antonio, 14,500; St. Ann's Bay, 11,900; Morant Bay, 9,900; and Ocho Rios, 9,300.

People in Cities

More than half of Jamaica's population (55 percent) lives in urban areas. The Kingston Metropolitan Area (KMA)— St. Catherine parish and Montego Bay, are the largest and second-largest urban concentrations.

Kingston Metropolitan Area and St. Catherine

The Kingston Metropolitan Area (KMA) contains the parishes of Kingston and St. Andrew. Portmore and Spanish Town, both large towns, are located in nearby St. Catherine parish. Kingston's metropolitan area is made up of 83 communities, approximately 63 percent of which display inner-city characteristics. As the capital of Jamaica, Kingston has a wide sphere of national and international influence. The KMA is the chief center for manufacturing, commerce, government, and finance, and it has the main transport terminus for the country. The University of Technology and the main campus of the University of the West Indies (in the suburb of Mona) are both located in the KMA. KMA is also rich with cultural history, theaters, art galleries, and museums and is home to some of Jamaica's wealthiest people. It is the center of innovative music and entertainment businesses, and its world-famous music studios have produced new forms of music such as ska, reggae, and rocksteady.

Kingston is built around Kingston Harbor, the island's main port. The Norman Manley International Airport is located on the Palisadoes strip, providing international and local connections. At one time, railroads connected Kingston

Kingston is the capital of Jamaica and heart of island life. The sprawling metropolitan area is made up of 83 communities that are rich with cultural history. This craft market is just one of the many venues for Jamaicans to come together and share their crafts and culture.

with Montego Bay, Port Antonio, and Ewarton, but those railroads are no longer operational. Traffic in the KMA is heavy and congested as people move in and out of Kingston. Some Jamaicans commute to work from the opposite side of the island over dangerous mountain roads. Roads crossing the island are narrow, winding, and full of potholes, and traffic is heavy and drivers are impatient (to put it mildly!).

Montego Bay

Montego Bay, or Mo Bay, as it is popularly known, is deservedly one of the most famous tourist destinations in the world. Over the years, it has attracted the rich and the famous

Montego Bay is on the northwestern coast and is a gateway for tourist travel. Sam Sharpe Square is a cobblestone square named after a national hero. Sam Sharpe was a slave and Baptist deacon who advocated passive resistance to the planters during the nineteenth century. He was hanged in the square and after independence the square was renamed for him.

and has been the vacation spot for royalty. It is also an important seaport and commercial center and the capital of St. James Parish. In 1981, Montego Bay was given the legal status of "city," thereby joining Kingston as the country's second community to receive this distinction. It lies on the northwestern coast and is the gateway for tourist travel on the north and west sides of the island. Montego Bay means "Lard Bay," as translated from the Spanish *Bahia de Manteca.*

The commercial area of Montego Bay's free port lay dormant for almost two decades but now is growing rapidly as the home of garment factories and electronic information companies. Port facilities continue to be underutilized, mostly serving cruise ships. A multimillion-dollar cruise ship terminal and shopping center was recently completed, making Montego Bay a welcoming port of call for any number of cruise lines.

Jamaica's overall pattern of settlement is one of virtually no increase within the rural areas and of increasing urban growth. The larger urban areas are tending to sprawl and expand into rural ones, and formerly rural areas are acquiring urban characteristics. Some urban to rural migration (reverse migration) is occurring as people who migrated to Kingston and St. Catherine have begun returning to their home parishes.

Rural Settlement

Traditional island life was rural. Scattered farmhouses, villages, and very small towns found in the countryside are all examples of rural settlements. Many Jamaicans still live in these types of settlements, which are built around activities such as agriculture and fishing. A cluster of houses with a population of approximately 500 is considered a village. In Jamaica, a village is also called a district. A few houses scattered over a wide area is a dispersed settlement pattern. There are many of these in the hilly limestone interior and in the Blue Mountains.

Social structure in Jamaica is unlike the pattern of social organization associated with many developing countries, because there are no clans, lineage, or traditional village leaders. The largest grouping of family households is at the district level.

OUT OF MANY, ONE PEOPLE

The Jamaican national motto, "Out of many, one people," reflects the ethnic diversity that is Jamaican society and the national pride that unifies its citizens. The people of Jamaica come from many different backgrounds, and most citizens are a mix of several different ethnicities. What defines Jamaica is the merging of cultural traditions and economic practices from Europe and Africa, and, to a lesser extent, Asia. From Great Britain, Jamaica inherited language, a system of government and justice, Christianity, and in a lesser sense, forms of architecture. From Africa came a tradition rich in folklore, music, magic, and a strong belief in religion. The remainder of island's rich and varied culture is exclusively Jamaican. Unique religions, music, foods, and art forms have developed on the island and, in some cases, have spread through the Caribbean and overseas to influence other cultures.

ETHNIC GROUPS

The great majority of Jamaicans are descendents of African slaves. Breakdown of population by ethnic group shows that 90.9 percent is African, 1.3 percent is East Indian, 0.2 percent is European, 0.2 percent is Chinese, 7.3 percent is of mixed ethnicity, and 0.1 percent is other ethnic groups. Jamaicans take pride in their African heritage and its expression in language, religion, food, music, and literature. A number of traits and practices directly traceable to Africa are observed today in Maroon and Kumina communities. They are expressed through local stories, songs, dances, the use of herbs and bush medicines, local beliefs, the preparation of indigenous foods, and religious practices.

Maroon Communities

Descendents of Maroons still live in Jamaica. Maroons are a mix of Africans who came to Jamaica with the Spanish and survived the English conquest and runaway British slaves who later joined with Maroons. Maroons became a nation within a nation and still maintain many of the old traditions. For example, the Accompong Maroons gather every year to celebrate "The Day," January 6, when Kojo, leader of the Maroons, routed the British forces in 1736. It is said that anyone who knows West Africa would find signs of Africa clearer in the Maroon villages

On January 6, 2002, the Accompong Maroons gathered to celebrate the day Kojo, then leader of the Maroons, routed the British forces in 1736. This photograph shows the 264th annual Accompong Maroon Festival. Here, Colonel Sidney Peddie is flanked by Maroons wearing traditional warrior dress.

than anywhere else in the West Indies. Many of the Maroons were Koromanti, people from the Akan region of West Africa, now known as Ghana. Although Maroon culture is not uniformly a product of Akan origins, there are extensive Ghanian influences. The Maroon communities today are Accompong, home to the Leeward Maroons, in the western Cockpit Country and Moore Town, Scotts Hall, and Charles Town, villages of the Windward Maroons, in the eastern Blue Mountains.

Granny Nanny of the Maroons

Nanny of the Maroons is a Jamaican national hero, and her story is immortalized in legend and song. Nanny was a leader of the Eastern Maroons. During the First Maroon War, she became—both during her lifetime and after—a symbol of unity and strength for her people during times of crisis. She was a small wiry woman with piercing eyes. Her influence over the Maroons was so strong that it seemed to be supernatural and was said to be connected to her powers of obeah (a religion similar to African voodoo). She was particularly skilled at organizing guerrilla warfare, which kept British troops from penetrating Maroon strongholds in the mountains. Besides being a fierce warrior, Nanny was a chieftainess, or a wise woman of the village, who passed down legends and kept African customs, music, and songs alive.

Kumina Sect

The Kumina are both a people and spiritual tradition. They are thought to be descended from Congolese indentured workers and freed slaves, and they survive in eastern parts of the island. This is the most African of the cults to be found in Jamaica, with little European or Christian influence. Kumina ceremonies are usually associated with wakes, burials, or memorial services but also can be performed for births, thanksgivings, and invocations for good and evil. Kumina sessions, which involve singing, dancing, and drumming, are of two general types: a public, less sacred form of Kumina, in which songs are sung mainly in Jamaican patois (dialect or provincial speech), and the more African and serious form (*pukumina,* the ritual of *pocomania,* meaning "small madness").

LANGUAGE

English is the official language of the country and the language taught in the schools, but most Jamaicans speak English and a patois. Jamaican patois, sometimes just called Jamaican, is an English-based creole language (a language that evolved from a combination of others and that serves as the native language of a community) with West African grammar

For a small country, Jamaica has a wide diversity of religious expression. The variety of houses of worship ranges from this traditional church to the bamboo shacks of the Revivalists.

and words from English, West African, Spanish, French, and Native American sources. It is spoken in the home and in other informal settings. Jamaican speech, whether in English or patois, has a distinctive rhythmic and melodic quality.

RELIGION

It is said that there are more churches per square mile in Jamaica than anywhere else in the world. The variety of houses of worship covers everything from centuries-old parish churches to the bamboo and zinc shacks of Revivalists. The majority (61.3 percent) of believers belong to one of the numerous Christian denominations—the Church of God, Baptists, Anglicans, Seventh-Day Adventists, Pentecostals, and Roman Catholics predominate, along with Methodists, United

Church, Moravians, Mennonites, Plymouth Brethren, Unity, and Jehovah's Witnesses. Other religious groups include Jews, Hindus, Muslims, and Bahais, and not least Rastafarians. Few countries in the world can match Jamaica's religious diversity, particularly considering the country's small size and population.

Rastafarianism

Rastafarianism is a religious movement that began in the 1930s in poor sections of Kingston and other Jamaican cities. It emerged out of biblical prophecy as interpreted by the political aspirations and teachings of Marcus Mosiah Garvey, a native Jamaican. Garvey taught that people of African descent will find peace, dignity, self-expression, and self-reliance by embracing Africa as their ancestral home. Rastafarians believe that black people are the descendents of the early Israelites who were sent into exile. They honor Haile Selassie (Ras Tafari), a former emperor of Ethiopia. His lineage, believe the Rastafarians, can be traced back to King Solomon and the Queen of Sheba. They believe, as did Selassie, himself, that he was "King of Kings, Lord of Lords, and Conquering Lion of the tribe of Judah."

Dreadlocked hair symbolizes the Lion of Judah and rebellion against Babylon, which is often equated to Western civilization. Followers of Rastafarianism understand Babylon as representing the artificial affluent society of self-absorbed individuals who worship idols and live decadent lifestyles at the expense of the poor. The wearing of dreadlocks has become closely associated with the movement, although the practice is not universal among, or exclusive to, Rastas.

Rastafarians believe that smoking *ganja* (marijuana) has Biblical approval, as well as being an aid to meditation and a form of religious observance. The colors red, green, and gold are sacred to the Rastafarian religion and frequently appear on clothing and other decorations. Most Rastas follow a certain diet, and some are vegetarians. They eat food that has not been contaminated by modern chemicals, salt, or preservatives. Restricted food items include alcohol, coffee, milk, and soft drinks. Anything that is herbal, such as tea, is acceptable.

There are a number of different Rastafarian sects that adhere to greater or lesser degrees to the beliefs of orthodox Rastafarianism. About 700,000 people practice the faith worldwide; this growth is largely attributed to Bob Marley, reggae artists, and the worldwide acceptance of reggae as an avenue of Rastafarian self-expression. Today, about 300,000 people, or 1 in 12 Jamaicans, consider themselves Rastafarians or Rasta sympathizers. The influence of Rastas in Jamaica has always outweighed their numbers, especially with respect to popular culture (in music, clothing styles, and speech).

FOOD

Jamaican foods represent a blending of many food traditions, from African to Amerindian, and Asian to European. Most foods and methods of preparation evolved from conditions of slavery and its aftermath to form a distinct dietary tradition, much of which is unique to Jamaica. Jamaica has an especially wide range of food as compared with the other English-speaking islands in the Caribbean. Much of Jamaican food is highly spiced and can be made even hotter by adding scotch bonnet pepper sauce. Rice, vegetables (such as yams, peas, tomatoes, hot peppers, and green peppers), fruit (such as mangoes, bananas, papayas, pineapples, oranges, and grapefruits), stews, chicken, and various types of fish (salt- and freshwater) figure largely in the diet. Fish may be eaten two or more times a week. Ackee and saltfish is Jamaica's national dish; it can be eaten both as breakfast and as a main course and is often accompanied by bammies (cassava or manioc bread), johnnycakes, avocado, fried plantains, yams, or roasted breadfruit.

A popular way of preparing fresh fish is to escoveitch them. Would you like to try one of Jamaica's most popular dishes?

JAMAICAN ESCOVEITCH FISH RECIPE

Ingredients:

    2 lb any whole small fish or filets

    1 lime

    ¼ cup flour, seasoned with salt and pepper

    oil for frying

    1 cup white or cider vinegar

    1 cup water

    pinch of salt; pinch of sugar

    1 cup julienned strips of carrot and choco (chayote, available
       at Hispanic markets; you can substitute zucchini)

    1 large hot pepper, such as scotch bonnet, cut in rings

    1 large onion, cut in rings

    6 pimento (allspice) berries

After fish are washed, squeeze lime into rinse water to reduce fishy taste. Dust with flour, fry, and set aside.

Boil together water, vinegar, sugar, and salt. Add the remaining ingredients and cook briefly. Pour sauce over fish and leave to marinate in refrigerator 4 to 24 hours before serving.

Most meals are served with rice and "peas" (red beans) and may also include boiled green bananas, plantains, or fried dumplings. Stews, thick soups, and curries are popular. One-pot meals include pepper pot soup, gungo pea stew, beef soup, red pea soup, and fricasseed chicken. Curried goat is a common party food, and leftover parts are used to make mannish water, a delicacy. Jerk is a favorite of Jamaicans and visitors alike. Jerk is spicy barbequed pork or chicken roasted in open pits or on makeshift grills. Bammy is a common food and is still prepared in the style of the Taino Indians. Bammy with fried fish is a frequent combination, as is festival (fried dough) with fish. Drinks made from boiled roots, herbal teas, fruit juices, and a variety of alcoholic drinks are common, as are coffee and tea. (All hot drinks are called "tea.")

The role of ackee, rice, and saltfish in the Jamaican diet

Ackee and saltfish is Jamaica's national dish and can be eaten for breakfast or for a main course. Ackee is a fruit that is not native to the country; it was imported from West Africa, probably aboard a slave ship.

has an interesting history. In fact, a famous Jamaican folk song, *Jamaican Farewell*, has in its lyrics, "Ackee, rice, saltfish are nice . . ." How did these three nonnative foods become so popular? During the early stages of the sugar plantation economy, all available productive land was devoted to growing that lucrative crop. The ackee, native to Africa, is a tree that can grow in very thin, rocky soil and thrive. It could be planted on poor land unsuited to the growing of cane. Rice was grown in abundance in British Asian colonies. Once dried, it can last almost indefinitely, even in the hot, humid, tropical climate. Plantation owners certainly were not going to send slaves to sea in boats to fish, so they had to turn elsewhere—to the British-controlled Grand Banks, rich fishing grounds off the coast of eastern Canada—for meat. Here, codfish were plentiful. How could their flesh be preserved and sent to a tropical land? The answer was found in salt drying the fish—this became a Caribbean delicacy still enjoyed today!

In rural areas, families eat dinner together each day after 4:00 P.M. Families in urban areas may eat together only on weekends. Tradition dictates that the family shares a meal on Sunday. Even poor families have a sociable midday meal, usually including chicken, fish, yams, fried plantains, and nearly always peas and rice. Eating outdoors, especially in gardens and on patios, is popular. Restaurants range from informal cafés that serve simple Jamaican dishes to restaurants offering a variety of dishes. Indian and Chinese foods are popular. Both shops and street vendors sell take-away foods. Pineapples, melons, and water coconuts (immature coconuts) are often sold from roadside stalls or carts. Patty shops are like hamburger stands in the United States. Patties, mixtures of spicy beef, curried lobster, or chicken wrapped in deep-fried curry-seasoned pastry, are Jamaica's fast food.

FOLKLORE AND BELIEFS

Many present-day oral traditions can be traced to folklore that has been passed down from the earliest African slaves. There are two spirits in Jamaican folklore, Obeah and Jumbie. Obeah is a superstitious spirit that is held accountable for both good and evil. According to legend, Obeah takes things away from people who take such things as happiness, health, love, and wealth for granted. When a Jamaican is asked "How are you feeling," he or she may answer, "Could be better," or "Not too bad." The jumbie is common to a number of Caribbean islands. They are said to be the spirits of people who have died, but do not want to leave their island. Jumbies are represented at Carnival and other parades by 12 to18 foot (3.5 to 5.5 meters) tall, stilt-walking revelers twirling Mocko Jumbies.

Anancy Stories

Jamaican lore is full of stories of the West African–linked Anancy. Anancy, the "Spiderman," is of Ashanti (Ghanese tribe) origin. Every Jamaican has memories of Anancy stories, from *Anancy and Dawg* to *Pig an Long-Mout,* as told by an elder family member or friend. Anancy stories are parables, tales used to teach lessons. In Jamaica, the spider-god has become a "spider man" who walks upright and is a cunning trickster. He always gets whatever he wants, but his quest always carries a good lesson.

Anancy is a rebellious spirit. He has the power to overturn the social order. According to legend, he can marry the king's daughter, create wealth out of thin air, baffle the devil, and even cheat death. Should Anancy lose in one tale, you know that he will surely overcome adversity in the next. Anancy conveyed a simple message, passed from one generation to the next of an oppressed people: freedom and dignity are worth fighting for, regardless of the consequences.

JAMAICAN PERSONALITY

Jamaicans, in general, are a friendly and outgoing people. They enjoy swapping stories and good humor (or "liming," as it is called). Jamaicans also have a positive and carefree attitude toward life. Many questions or situations are answered with a "No problem, mon!" in the belief that things will work out fine. Many Jamaicans are very talented, often quite opinionated, and are very proud of their country and its people.

5

Administration and Government

Jamaica is a democratic country but one beset with many problems. This chapter describes and explains the country's governance, its divisions, and the problems it faces in serving its people.

COUNTIES AND PARISHES

Jamaica is divided into three counties, each of which is further divided into parishes. In the mid-nineteenth century, Jamaica had a total of 22 parishes. Now there are only 14. Each parish has a capital, which is the site of its local government. Kingston, the capital of Kingston-Port Royal, is also the seat of government for the country. The counties are

- Surrey, 820 square miles (2,124 square kilometers), the eastern county, which includes the parishes of Kingston-Port Royal (capital: Kingston), St. Andrew (capital:

Half–Way Tree), St. Thomas (capital: Morant Bay), and Portland (capital: Port Antonio);

- Middlesex, 2,026 square miles (5,248 square kilometers), the middle county, which includes the parishes of St. Catherine (capital: Spanish Town), St. Mary (capital: Port Maria), Clarendon (capital: May Pen), St. Ann (capital: St. Ann's Bay), and Manchester (capital: Mandeville); and

- Cornwall, 1,565 square miles (4,053 square kilometers), the western county, which contains St. Elizabeth (capital: Black River), Trelawny (capital: Falmouth), St. James (capital: Montego Bay), Hanover (capital: Lucea), and Westmoreland (capital: Savanna-la-Mar).

GOVERNMENT

Politically, Jamaica suffers from the same problems that do many less developed countries (LDCs). Considering its diverse populations, poverty, differences in political ideology, and many other problems, the country can take considerable pride in the fact that it has been able to maintain a relatively stable government.

Jamaica became an independent country on August 6, 1962. It is also member of the British Commonwealth. The government is a constitutional monarchy, with the British crown represented on the island by a governor general. The governor general appoints the prime minister who, in turn, recommends ministers who make up the cabinet. The prime minister and ministers come from the political party that holds the majority in the country's parliament. Elections are held every five years.

There are two houses of Parliament. The House of Representatives (60 seats) consists of elected representatives who serve five-year terms. The Senate (21 seats) is appointed by the prime minister and the leader of the opposition. The government is headed by the prime minister, who is required to consult with

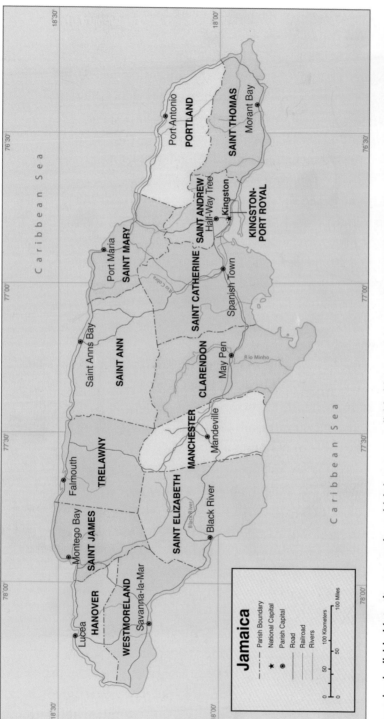

Jamaica is divided into three counties, which in turn are divided into parishes. In the mid-nineteenth century Jamaica had 22 parishes, but today it has only 14. Each parish has a capital, which is the site of its local government.

the governor general and the leader of the opposition on certain matters.

POLITICAL PARTIES

Jamaica has three major political parties. They are the Jamaican Labour Party (JLP), the People's National Party (PNP), and the more recently formed National Democratic Movement (NDM). The popularity of the Workers Party of Jamaica, a small Communist party, formerly led by university professor Trevor Munroe, is fading. The JLP generally favors private enterprise, whereas the PNP advocates moderate socialism. The PNP is the current ruling party, with 35 seats in the House of Representatives (after the 2002 election). Percival James Patterson, leader of the PNP, has been prime minister since 1992.

Jamaica Labour Party

William Alexander Bustamante, a businessman and labor leader, formed the Jamaica Labour Party in 1943. The JLP was elected to govern in the first election held under the 1944 constitution, which granted universal adult suffrage. Subsequently, the party was elected to office in 1949 to 1955, 1962 to 1972, and 1980 to 1989. The party's current leader is Edward Seaga. The JLP is considered to be Jamaica's more conservative and consistent party. For example, it has always promoted the free market system and during the 1970s and 1980s, it was strongly pro-U.S. and vehemently anti-Communist.

People's National Party

The People's National Party (PNP) was formed in 1938. Norman Washington Manley, an attorney, became its first leader soon afterward. Manley, who died in 1969, is now regarded as a national hero. The PNP formed the government from 1955 to 1962, 1972 to 1980, and 1989 to 1992. Under the leadership of Michael Manley (son of Norman Manley), the

Prime Minister Percival J. Patterson signals to his supporters during the October elections in 2002. He won his third term of office as a result of this election.

party promoted "democratic socialism" and aligned Jamaica closely with Cuba's Fidel Castro. The current party leader, attorney Percival J. Patterson, is a strong supporter of the free market system.

TRADE UNION MOVEMENT

The trade union movement has grown rapidly. In 1996, there were more than 85 registered trade unions. The main function of the trade union is to act as mediator between employer and employee. The Trade Union Act of 1919 made it possible to form, register, and operate trade unions in Jamaica. It was not until 1938, a time of high unemployment, low wages, and widespread riots, that the first lasting trade unions were formed. They were closely linked with political parties. Alexander Bustamante organized the first union, the Bustamante Industrial Trade Union (BITU), in 1939. This union became affiliated with the JLP. The president of the BITU, former Prime Minister Hugh Shearer, only recently resigned as deputy leader of the Jamaica Labor Party. The Trade Union Congress formed in 1949, followed by the National Workers Union; both were linked to the PNP. The National Workers Union was founded out of a split between the PNP and the Trade Union Congress (TUC) in 1952.

The two dominant trade unions are the BITU and NWU. BITU was formed out of five labor unions, with Bustamante the head of each. The unions represented maritime workers, transport labor, factory workers, municipal employees, and general labor. A few months after the formation of the five unions, Bustamante gave up the idea of a group of unions because of organizational difficulties and instead merged them into a single all-inclusive labor organization named after himself and designating him as president for life.

The NWU started its activities in labor representation by organizing and eventually controlling the bauxite industry. It began with Noel Nethersole as president and Florizel Glasspole as general secretary. Michael Manley, the son of Norman Manley, was one of their assistants. Since then, other unions that are not connected to political parties have been formed. The first of these was the University and Allied Workers Union (UAWU) established by Trevor Munroe.

EDUCATION SYSTEM

Jamaica's education system is based on the British system. Primary education covers six years from age six to age twelve (grades 1 to 6). It is free and compulsory (mandatory). At the end of this cycle, pupils sit for the National Assessment Programme (NAP), which is the basis of selection for secondary education. Secondary education covers five years (grades 7 to 11) with an additional two years (grades 12 and 13) for those who wish to proceed to higher education.

Secondary Education

Secondary education is available through a system of public and private schools. Government-sponsored scholarships for public secondary schools are awarded on the basis of a student's success in the National Assessment Programme (NAP) exams. Children not admitted into government-aided secondary schools can obtain a secondary education at one of several private schools. Unfortunately, in terms of the country's potential human resources, approximately one-third of Jamaica's young people do not go on to secondary education.

High schools are quite selective. They provide a maximum seven-year program leading to the Caribbean Examinations Council Secondary Education Certificate after five years (grade 11) and GCE Advanced "A" levels after another two years (grade 13). New secondary schools provide a five-year course. After four years, pupils may take the Jamaica School Certificate (grade 10), and the course usually leads to receipt of a Secondary School Certificate (grade 11).

School Day and Calendar

School generally starts early in the morning between 7:30 and 8:00 and runs until about 2:00 in the afternoon. Sessions are broken with both a morning and lunch break. Some schools operate on a shift system, with an additional set of students arriving in the afternoon. Students wear uniforms to school, whether in grade 1, technical school, or college. Boys are always in white or khaki shirts and khaki pants. Girls are usually in white shirts, but each school chooses its own color and style of dress or tunic. The streets literally become a rainbow of colors as students make their way to and from school.

There are three school terms for the year:

- September to December

- January to April

- May to July

Mid-term breaks are of one to two weeks around National Heroes Day (the third Monday in October), Ash Wednesday, and Easter (Good Friday/Easter Monday). Schools set their own term dates, but they differ only slightly.

Subjects

Teams of teachers, education officers, and Jamaican and international consultants develop the curriculum in response to national goals and student needs. The primary school curriculum covers language, mathematics, science, social studies, drama, music, visual arts, physical education, and religious education. At secondary level public schools, the curriculum is centered around five core subjects: language arts, mathematics, resources and technology, science, and social studies.

Universities

Jamaica is home to the main campus of the University of the West Indies (UWI), a regional institution with campuses also in Jamaica, Barbados, and Trinidad. The Mona campus is located in a Kingston suburb and is the site of the university's central administration. The University of Technology, Jamaica (UTech), formerly the College of Arts, Science, and Technology (CAST), is Jamaica's only national university. It is also located in Kingston. UTech was given university status in September 1995. Agricultural studies, science, and education are taught at the College of Agriculture, Science, and Education (CASE), located on the northeast side of the island in Portland parish. The college has its roots in the Government Farm School in Kingston, which first opened its doors in 1910. At its inception, the school's goal was to train the approximately 12 young men enrolled at the time the "art and science of agriculture." In its first decade, the school produced leaders such as the late Dr. T. P. Lecky, a Jamaican animal scientist who developed the Jamaica Hope and Jamaica Black breeds of cattle.

HEALTH CARE

For a developing country, Jamaicans generally enjoy good health. In 1966, the government began one of the world's first national health services. Government clinics have provided preventative care and medical treatment ever since. Additionally, government-supported inoculation programs and investments to improve sanitation have reduced many diseases.

For many years, government-operated public hospitals and clinics provided free Western-style medical care. Since the 1980s, however, government support of public health and social services has declined because of the island's economic problems. A growing number of private hospitals and clinics now provide good health care, but at a cost. Today, health care is quite expensive and understaffed clinics and hospitals have long lists of patients waiting for treatment. Nearly all drugs must be imported and are very costly.

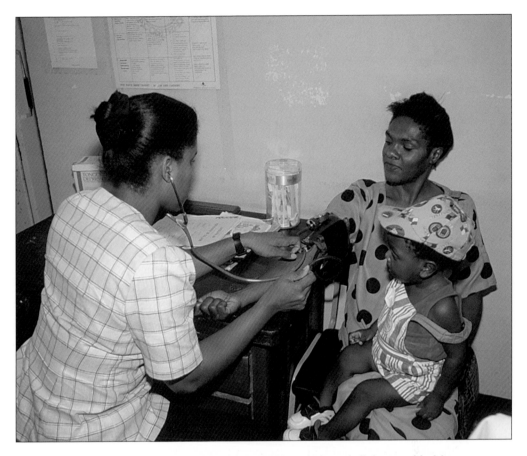

For many years government-operated hospitals and clinics provided free medical care. Today, the health care and social services have declined along with the failing economy, but rural clinics such as this one still provide services, but at a cost.

Because the country's medical care is so costly, many Jamaicans now rely on traditional remedies, going to a doctor only as a last resort. Jamaicans use fruits and vegetables for their healing properties. Papaya helps relieve indigestion, guava leaves treat diarrhea, and tamarind soothes itchy skin and chicken pox. Herbal medicines are popular. "Balmists" (rural "folk" doctors), who practice "bush medicine," provide treatment for a wide range of ailments. Herbs, such as a tea, a poultice, or a bath, are administered. One popular folk remedy is bush tea, a concoction that contains ingredients such as lemon, fevergrass, soursop, breadfruit leaves, and pepper elder. Herbs, with colorful names such as *search-mi-heart* and *shame o' lady,* are popular treatments for colds and stomach ailments. *Ganja* (marijuana) is boiled into a tea for asthma and eye complaints. The *cerassee* vine is used as a general health booster and is sold in teabags. This may sound primitive, but it is important to remember that nearly one-half of the pharmaceuticals marketed in the United States come from plant or animal extracts.

PORTS, AIRPORTS, AND ROADS

Jamaica has two world-class international seaports: the Port of Kingston and Port of Montego Bay. Kingston's transshipment port underwent expansion in 2001 to increase docking capacity for ships. The bauxite/alumina industry and agricultural exporters use smaller, specialized ports. Cruise ship facilities in Ocho Rios and Montego Bay were recently upgraded, and the government has announced plans to upgrade facilities at Port Antonio, including construction of a large yacht basin.

If you were flying from the United States to Jamaica, you would probably enter the country through one of two international airports: Norman Manley International Airport in Kingston or Sangster International Airport in Montego Bay. Air connections from these airports to smaller airports located in Mandeville, Negril, Ocho Rios, and Port Antonio are available.

Roads crisscross the island and are major routes of travel for Jamaicans. The highway system, consisting of 10,000 miles of primary and secondary roads, is badly outdated and in disrepair. The author of this book once spent nearly six hours crossing the island on a 25-mile trip, which, should have taken no more than 30 minutes! The first phase of the North Coast highway project (linking the major coastal tourist areas of Montego Bay and Negril) began in 1999 but has not made much progress. Driving can be a very scary experience in

Jamaica: The country uses the British system of vehicles with the driver in the right side driving on the left side of the road, and few drivers seem to obey the traffic laws. The roads are cluttered with animals, pedestrians, carts, abandoned vehicles, and potholes. The country has a very high fatality rate considering the miles driven.

CHAPTER

6

Economy

J amaica is classified as a less developed country (LDC), as is true of countries throughout the Caribbean and elsewhere in Latin America. The nation faces many problems that hinder economic growth. It also has many advantages that, if properly developed, can boost development.

IS JAMAICA A WEALTHY COUNTRY?

Gross domestic product (GDP) is one of several measures used to determine the wealth of a country and the health of its economy. GDP is defined as the market value of all property and all goods and services produced by labor within a country. Jamaica's GDP during the early years of the twenty-first century averaged approximately U.S. $7.5 to $8.0 billion. When converted to purchasing power parity (PPP)—that is, its equivalent to purchasing power in the United States—Jamaica's GDP was estimated at about U.S. $10.0 billion.

GDP divided by the total population is a measure called per capita GDP. During recent years, this has fluctuated between the U.S. equivalent of about $3,400 and $3,900. These and other indices place Jamaica in the category of a developing country, one whose economy has not fully matured.

Jamaica's GDP composition by sector was 63 percent in services, 31 percent in industry, and 6 percent in agriculture. During recent years, the three largest contributors to the GDP were tourism (15 percent), bauxite/alumina (10 percent), and manufactured products such as clothing, processed sugar, rum, and other beverages (17 percent).

ECONOMIC WOES

Jamaica has many economic concerns. Declines in the GDP, general lack of growth in most economic sectors and declines in others, and mounting debt are worrisome, as is the island's chronic problem of unemployment, which has been averaging about 15 percent. That figure would be more than doubled, however, if underemployment—people in low-paying jobs—was considered. At the end of September 2002, the public debt was U.S. $10.7 billion, or 130 percent of the GDP. Debt servicing accounted for 45 percent of the 2002–2003 budget. Most of this debt was acquired during years when the government borrowed huge amounts of money to develop the bauxite industry and expand tourism.

Imports and Foreign Exchange

Both GDP and foreign exchange inflows in Jamaica are sensitive to changes in the global economy. They are particularly vulnerable to whatever is happening to the U.S. economy. Less prosperous times in the United States translate to near-depression in Jamaica, with many people out of work. The country needs foreign exchange (non-Jamaican currency) to buy imported goods. Jamaican currency is the Jamaican dollar. Today it takes 50 Jamaican dollars to make 1 U.S. dollar. Like most island countries, Jamaica is dependent on trade to supply many of its basic needs. Imports of goods and services totaled an estimated

$3.1 billion in 2001, which is a sizable percentage of the GDP. Of this amount, most was spent on machinery, transport equipment, fuels, manufactured goods, and food.

Foreign Ownership

The government controls some key industries, but there are many foreign-owned companies, especially those controlling exports (bauxite/alumina) and tourism, the most important foreign exchange earners.

TOURISM—JAMAICA'S LEADING INDUSTRY

Without a doubt, tourism is Jamaica's number one industry. It is the largest foreign exchange earner, a major contributor to the GDP, one of Jamaica's fastest-growing industries, and the country's second-largest employer. Tourism began in Jamaica in the 1890s. The American-owned United Fruit Company created this industry by using the extra space on its banana boats to encourage tourist cruises to Jamaica. In response to the increased need in facilities, tourist hotels were constructed on the island. Tourism, however, did not really begin to flourish until the mid—twentieth century, particularly after World War II. Port Antonio, located on the island's north coast, was Jamaica's first tourist resort and for many years a favorite retreat for writers and artists, including Ian Fleming, creator of James Bond. Additional hotel incentive legislation passed in 1968 continued to transform the industry and eventually strengthened the role of larger, often foreign-owned hotels and resorts.

Jamaica is the fifth most popular tourist destination in the Caribbean. The island has many attractions for tourists: scenic beauty; a warm, sunny climate; beautiful beaches; and a unique culture, as well as the warmth and friendliness of its people. Jamaica's location close to the United States and Canada make it easy and relatively inexpensive for visitors from these countries to visit Jamaica.

Tourism is Jamaica's number one industry. The town of Ocho Rios was once a fishing village, but today it welcomes thousands of tourists who arrive in huge cruise ships.

Types of Tourism

What is tourism? By definition it is an industry, usually called a service industry, that caters to the needs of visitors. Tourism is described as the world's largest and fastest-growing industry. Today, people travel for a variety of reasons: relaxation, adventure, nature, history, and culture. For many years, Jamaican tourism has centered on the hotel complexes of the northern and western coasts and the cruise ship ports of call at Montego Bay and Ocho Rios. New types of tourism are extending tourist activities to other parts of the country. Cultural-heritage tourism, sustainable tourism (ecotourism), and special event tourism are showing especially strong growth. What is really meant by cultural-heritage tourism, sustainable tourism, and special event tourism?

Cultural-Heritage Tourism

Some tourists travel to learn about the culture and history of places other than where they live. Jamaica has a colorful culture in which visitors may experience new foods, music, sports, dance, and drama. Until recently, few sites had been developed for the cultural-heritage tourist. Now, popular historical attractions include sites such as Port Royal and Spanish Town, the Taino Museum at White Marl (St. Catherine), and the great plantation houses that are scattered throughout the island. Jamaica-based companies offer tours of working plantations, small farms, and both urban and rural communities.

Sustainable Tourism/Ecotourism

Sustainable tourism, also called ecotourism, is a relatively new concept. Ecotourism promotes the use of land, water, plants, and other resources in their natural states. It provides a unique visitor experience with minimal negative impact on the environment and local communities. Blue and John Crow Mountains National Park, established in 1993, has a number of ecotourism projects, in which community involvement is a high priority.

Special Event Tourism

Often, tourists visit a place for a special event. Jamaica has music events such as Reggae Sunsplash, Reggae Sumfest, and Jamaica Carnival and sporting events such as golf tournaments, test cricket, and fishing tournaments.

Tourist Arrivals

There are two categories of tourists in Jamaica: cruise ship visitors and those staying in hotels, guesthouses, and apartments. Jamaica recorded 2,131,785 visitor arrivals in 2002. Stopover visitors numbered 1,266,366, and cruise ship passengers totaled 865,419.

Cruise Ship Visitors

Cruise ship visitors come by the hundreds to a port where they spend only a few hours or at most a day or two. When they spend more than one day, they sleep aboard the ship. Montego Bay and Ocho Rios have developed extensive portside facilities to support cruise ship arrivals. The approach to Ocho Rios is especially beautiful, with five waterfalls visible from five miles (eight kilometers) out at sea as well as a view of the town, surrounded by lush tropical woodlands. Restaurants, craft vendors, tour operators, and craft shops are all within walking distance of the port. Many tourists take the short taxi ride to nearby Dunns River Falls recreational park. At this well-known attraction, visitors can climb the falls, enjoy the park, or relax on the beach.

Stopover Tourists

Stopover tourists occupy the more than 24,000 rooms at hotels, resort cottages, and apartments for days or weeks at a time. The majority of these tourists come from the United States, and others from Canada, the United Kingdom and elsewhere in Europe and, to a lesser extent, Japan and Latin America. Negril, little more than a fishing village attractive to a handful of hippies, Rastafarians, and musicians in the 1960s, has become Jamaica's third-greatest tourist destination. It is reputed to generate more income than either of the other two major resort areas, Montego Bay and Ochos Rios. Centered on Negril, the resort area stretches along the seven-mile beach strip in Long and Bloody bays and also along the cliffs at West End. It spans two parishes: Westmoreland and Hanover. Hotels and tourist businesses line the coast, and more developments are planned. Negril's main tourist attractions are a beautiful seven-mile white sand beach, rocky cliffs, spectacular sunsets, and reef diving. There are also many fine restaurants, as well as upscale inclusive resorts, hotels, villas, and apartments.

BAUXITE MINING AND REFINING

Bauxite mining and refining is the second-leading industry in Jamaica. Bauxite was first discovered and exploited in the 1940s. The subsequent establishment of the bauxite/alumina industry shifted Jamaica's economy away from its heavy emphasis on agricultural products (sugar and bananas).

Jamaica is the fourth-largest producer of bauxite ore, after Australia, Guinea, and Brazil, and it ranks third in the production of alumina. What is bauxite? How is it different from alumina? What makes the small country of Jamaica such an important producer? Bauxite is the ore from which the metal aluminum is extracted. In Jamaica, Haiti, and the Dominican Republic, it is red, rust-colored clay. In addition to containing aluminum, it also has a high percentage of iron. This bauxite is found exclusively in pockets on top of limestone. In Jamaica, it is associated with the white limestone that forms much of the island's hard rock surface layer.

Bauxite, like all ores, contains a limited amount of the required metal. The process of removing the aluminum is generally known as refining, and it is done in two stages. The first stage is to remove all the unwanted materials, such as iron oxides, and to obtain aluminum oxide, which is known as alumina. The alumina is further refined to produce aluminum. About two-thirds of Jamaica's bauxite is converted into alumina in local refineries and then shipped to smelters in the United States, Canada, and Norway, where aluminum is produced. Converting bauxite to alumina is an expensive process. It requires fuel and caustic soda, both of which are imported, plus the cost of building the refinery. Nevertheless, alumina is worth about ten times as much as bauxite and therefore is often considered worth the expense of producing it.

The Jamaican government has encouraged the development of alumina smelters on the island, but the last stage in smelting requires large amounts of direct electrical current. A small country like Jamaica cannot afford to build and fuel the large electrical power stations required to convert alumina to aluminum, so this process is carried out at plants outside Jamaica owned by industrial giants such as Alcan of Canada, Alcoa and Kaiser of the United States, and Hydro Aluminum of Norway. There are several reasons for Jamaica's high ranking as a bauxite/alumina producer: First is the quantity of ore and its suitability for mining; second, the commitment of the government and investors to development of the industry; and third, the close proximity of Jamaica to the United States, its major trading partner.

What are the prospects for the future of the Jamaican bauxite/alumina industry? Mining plays an essential role in the country's foreign exchange earnings (contributing about 60 percent toward foreign exchange earnings). Today, Jamaica's bauxite refineries are working at full capacity. It is estimated that the country's bauxite reserves will last another 50 to 100 years, with some estimates as long as 150 years. One huge environmental problem associated with the bauxite industry is the disposal of tailings. This waste material forms a sludge of alkaline mud. Jamaica's alumina-producing capacity is about three million tons a year. About one ton of red mud waste is created in the production of each ton of alumina. Jamaica's land area is quite limited. It therefore is difficult to accommodate the disposal of so much waste material. Sludge disposal is not the only problem. The residue that leaves the plant also has large amounts of weak caustic soda solution. Unsightly red "lakes" are formed by the present disposal processes.

AGRICULTURE FOR EXPORT AND LOCAL CONSUMPTION

Jamaica has a long and strong tradition of agriculture. The island's varied natural landscapes, climate, and soil provide a wide range of environmental conditions suited to a variety of crops. Farms of different sizes are found on flat alluvial plains, in the high areas of the Blue Mountains, in the limestone uplands and solution basins, and in the numerous river valleys.

Jamaican agriculture can be divided into three sectors: export crops, crops for local consumption, and livestock.

Export Crops

Agriculture for export has a long history. Like tourism, the bauxite/alumina industry and general manufacturing, it contributes substantially to the GDP, but more important, it is an earner of valued foreign exchange. Agriculture accounts for 7.4 percent of the country's GDP. Traditional agricultural exports are sugar, bananas, coffee, pimento (allspice), cocoa (chocolate), and fresh fruit. Large farms are called plantations or estates and often cover hundreds of acres (hectares) and grow a single crop. These estates are owned and operated by companies or families. They generally occupy alluvial (stream-deposited and therefore highly fertile) lands, although some extend into hilly areas. Coffee estates are the exception. The most highly prized coffee is grown at high elevations in the Blue Mountains. The main export crops today are sugar cane, bananas, coffee, cocoa (chocolate), citrus fruits, pimento (allspice), yams, and ornamentals (plants used for decoration).

Sugar Cane–Estate Agriculture

Sugar cane has been grown in Jamaica since 1509. In the sixteenth and seventeenth centuries, under the British plantation system, the island became the world's major producer and leading exporter of sugar and rum production reached 101,194 tons in 1805 but declined during the remainder of the century, finally reaching an all-time low of 4,969 tons in 1913. Factors in this drop included loss of labor with the abolition of slavery and growing competition from beet sugar. The all-time high of 514,825 tons was achieved in 1965. Production has declined steadily since then, to a 50-year record low of 152,161 tons in 2003.

Today, less land is planted with sugar cane, yields have dropped, and machinery in the sugar factories is aging. Jamaica does not produce enough sugar to meet its market demand and oddly enough is importing sugar for domestic consumption. The government hopes to reverse this trend through modernization of the factories and improved field practices. It plans to invest U.S. $100 million in the ailing sugar industry and has set a production target of 300,000 tons for 2004. Some of the most efficient sugar operations are those supplying the rum industry. Appleton Estates, operated by J. Wray and Nephew, Ltd., is said to be among the most modern plantations in the Caribbean. The Appleton distillery dates to the seventeenth century and produces the world-famous Appleton rum.

A number of significant changes have taken place in the industry during nearly five centuries of sugar production. Production methods have gone from the use of cheap slave (African) and indentured (East Indian and Chinese) labor to less labor and more capital-intensive methods. Despite industry declines in employment, sugar remains the largest single employer of labor in the agricultural sector, involving 50,000 people. The production of sugar cane was once confined to large plantations. Today, the huge estates must compete with some 12,000 independent cane farmers, who produce just over 50 percent of the cane processed.

The Banana Trade

Most bananas grown in the Caribbean are used at home, but Jamaica has a history of exporting them. Commercial banana trade began in 1900 and reached its peak in 1936, with 355,000 tons, of which 259,000 tons, or 73 percent, were shipped to the United Kingdom. About 10,800 acres (4,360 hectares) of land are now under production, with a banana export amounting to 86,074 tons in 1996.

Besides competition, the major inhibitor of the Jamaican banana industry has been hurricanes, with 16 occurrences since 1900. After Hurricane Allen in 1980, exports fell to a record low of 11,000 tons in 1984. Since then, Jamaica has carefully restructured the industry, with a focus on efficiency and productivity. Banana production and related activities are a source of 5 to 10 percent of total employment in the country.

Captain Lorenzo Dow Baker is often credited with developing the banana trade, and at the same time, he introduced tourism to the island. He was the founder of the Boston Fruit Company, which later merged with the United Fruit Company (UFCO). His banana boats not only carried cargo but also passengers to Port Antonio and other coastal towns. A tourist activity—still popular today—was rafting down the Rio Grande, which used the rafts made for transporting bananas from the estates to the ships on the coast. The banana trade began at the time sugar cane production was in its greatest decline. Old cane fields made ideal banana plantations. The trade flourished, particularly after the development of refrigerated service. The UFCO dominated the Jamaican trade until the late 1920s. The British government became worried about the increasing American influence on its Caribbean colony. It took action and began providing financial assistance to associations of banana growers who would supply the British market independently of the UFCO. This strategy was remarkably successful. Only World War II interrupted the steady flow of bananas to Great Britain.

Coffee

Coffee is a traditional export crop. Introduced to Jamaica in 1728, the coffee plant adapted easily to the country's mountainous terrain. Coffee declined as a major crop with the abolition of slavery but was revived in the mid-1950s with the formation of the Jamaican Coffee Industry Board (CIB). The Board worked to raise the standards of coffee production and established the first central factory (pulpery). The physical conditions for growing coffee in the Blue Mountains, coupled with the labor-intensive methods of cultivation and processing, have produced what many would call the finest coffee in world.

Jamaican Blue Mountain coffee beans have the reputation of being the world's highest grade and most expensive coffee. Coffee has been a traditional export crop since the late 1800s.

Jamaican Blue Mountain beans have the reputation of being the world's most expensive and highest grade of coffee—referred to as "the Rolls Royce of Coffee." Ironically, it is almost impossible to drink this wonderful coffee in any Jamaican restaurant.

Because of its value, in recent years, most of the small supply of Blue Mountain Coffee (80 percent) has been purchased prepaid by Japanese interests, with another 10 percent shipped to the United States.

Other Export Crops

Other export crops include cocoa, citrus, pimento, yams, and ornamentals or foliage. Pimento, although no longer a major crop in Jamaica, is one of its most unique. The pimento tree is native to the Caribbean. It was found growing in Jamaica by the early Spanish explorers, who were impressed by the taste and aroma of the berries and leaves. Most English-speaking people call the tree "pimento" and the berries "allspice." The name allspice comes from the idea that the pimento berry contains the characteristic flavor and aroma of cloves, cinnamon, nutmeg, and pepper all combined in one spice. Jamaica's allspice commands a premium price, although demand has declined. At the beginning of the twentieth century, Europe alone was using four times more allspice than is being produced today.

Crops for Local Consumption

Half of the agricultural land in Jamaica is owned or controlled by about 1,000 large estates or farms, and the remainder is divided among 185,000 or so small farms. Most Jamaican farms are quite small, less than five acres (two hectares). These farms employ the majority of farm labor and produce a wide range of crops, including some for export but mainly for the local market. Types of crops include roots, vegetables, fruits, and legumes. Shoppers in North America and European supermarkets will be familiar with some of the produce, but much of it will appear strange and exotic. Root crops or tubers, an important staple crop, include sweet potatoes, cassava, dasheen (also called taro), and especially a wide variety of yams. Popular vegetables include callaloo (a leafy green), green peppers, hot scotch bonnet peppers, tomatoes, cucumbers, corn, and pumpkin squash. Seasonal fruits include plantains, avocados, mangoes, pineapples, soursop, Otaheite apples (also called ambarella), ackee, breadfruit, jackfruit, and melons just to name a few. Legumes are commonly grown and include red peas (beans), gungo peas (pigeon peas), and peanuts.

Small-scale farming in Jamaica began during the period of slavery. Slaves who worked on the large plantations were given small plots called provision grounds. Here they were expected to grow a portion of their food supply, such as yams, cassava, and sweet potatoes, many of the same crops that are grown today. What they did not eat they were allowed to sell. Once a week there was Sunday market, with hundreds of people gathering to buy, sell, or trade livestock, vegetables, yams, and other foodstuffs, along with fruits and preserves and homemade mats, baskets, and ropes in a carnival-like atmosphere.

Bustling, crowded, noisy markets are very much a part of Jamaican life. American-style supermarkets with no-hassle parking offer just about every American product available, including familiar American fruits and vegetables. Local markets, however, are where one finds the wide array of fruits and vegetables so famous in the Caribbean. The local Saturday market is an institution in Jamaica. Higglers, the so-called vendors and marketers, form the backbone of the Jamaican internal marketing system. The word "higgler" comes from the verb to higgle, which is to haggle or bargain. Higglers direct market domestic crops to the public town market. They may come from the community of production, neighboring communities (country higglers), or even distant metropolitan areas (city higglers).

Several vegetables and fruits marketed locally bear special mention because of their importance in Jamaica's food traditions. Breadfruit and ackee have especially interesting histories.

Breadfruit

Breadfruit was unknown in Jamaica before 1793. The first attempt to introduce the breadfruit was made during a period of extreme food shortage. West Indian planters heard of a tree growing in distant Pacific Islands that provided "bread" year round. British sea captain, William Bligh, was appointed commander of an expedition to collect the plant. His ship was the *Bounty,* a name that would become famous in the annals of history. After obtaining plants from the small islands of Timor and Tahiti, Bligh and his crew set sail for the West Indies. On the return, the crew mutinied. The breadfruit plants were thrown overboard and Bligh was set adrift in the Pacific in a small open boat. Fortunately, Bligh survived this misfortune and decided to try again. His next attempt was successful. In 1793, sailing on the HMS *Providence,* he brought the first breadfruit plants to Jamaica and St. Vincent.

The introduction of the breadfruit tree was a great success. Not only does the tree bear a great abundance of fruit, but it also usually produces two crops a year. Breadfruit is a staple food item in the Jamaican diet.

Ackee

Ackee is the national fruit and an ingredient in the national dish, ackee and saltfish. While not native to Jamaica, ackee has remarkable historic associations. It was originally imported from West Africa, probably aboard a slave ship. In Jamaica, it thrives, producing large quantities of fruit each year. Ackee is edible, but only when fully ripe. Eating an ackee at the wrong stage of development can cause sickness, or even death.

Ackee was not recognized scientifically until Captain William Bligh (of "Mutiny on the Bounty" fame) took plants from Jamaica to England. In 1793, ackee was given the botanical name *Blighia sapida* in honor of the notorious sea captain. Today, even though the plant has been introduced into many

Jamaica is the only place in the islands where ackee is generally eaten as a food. Ackee is a fruit whose botanical name, *Blighia sapida*, was bestowed in 1793 in honor of the notorious sea captain William Bligh, who brought the fruit to England.

other Caribbean islands, Jamaica is the only place where the fruit is generally recognized as an edible crop.

Livestock

The Caribbean region is a major importer of food, meat and dairy products. Beef, in particular, is in especially short supply, which is why Jamaica plays such an important role in cattle raising. Jamaica has an active cattle-breeding program, which has crossbred larger, heavier English cattle with heat- and disease-resistant Indian cattle. The greatest success has been with the Jamaica Hope, a dairy animal, which is about 80 percent Jersey with 5 percent Holstein and only 15 percent

Indian zebu cattle. The main beef animal and the most common breed in Jamaica is the Jamaica Red, followed by the Jamaica Black, and Jamaica Brahman. The Jamaican cattle industry currently is able to produce about 80 percent of the beef and 14 percent of milk products consumed on the island.

Besides cattle, chickens, hogs, and goats are the main livestock animals reared on Jamaica. Chicken is Jamaica's most important source of animal protein. It is the cheapest meat, easy to cook, easily reared, and widely available. Fried chicken and jerk chicken are Jamaican favorites. Chicken is the meat source in which the island is most self-sufficient. Local supplies, however, are not enough. Chicken, especially chicken necks, backs, legs, and thighs, is imported. Pork is a popular meat, eaten as jerk pork, hot dogs, sausages, and ham. The parishes of Westmoreland and Hanover on west side of the island are the largest pork producers. Goats are raised for home consumption and the local market. Curried goat is a popular Jamaican dish, often featured at parties or large gatherings.

FISHERIES

Fish is a popular item in Jamaican diet. Most fishing has been to satisfy local needs, but in recent years, Jamaica has exported seafood. Conch (a shellfish) and lobster are the main exports. Most fish come from the sea, not from freshwater fisheries. The main fishing area is on the shallow waters of the continental shelf surrounding the island. King, snapper, grouper, dolphin, shark, barracuda, marlin, parrot fish, goatfish (red mullet), and jackfish are all found in Jamaica's waters.

FORESTRY AND FOREST INDUSTRIES

Jamaica's 500,000 hectares of forest play a critical role in the country's development. They provide lumber, posts, firewood, charcoal, fruits, medicinal plants, rope, drinks, and other consumables. They protect watersheds and therefore water supply, provide habitats for many wildlife species, and maintain soil productivity, and they are critical to Jamaica's scenic beauty. Managing forestlands is taken seriously. Commercial logging and other forest industries are tightly controlled. Hardwoods are in most demand, supporting subsidiary industries such as sawmills, treatment and planing plants, and furniture and craft workshops. Cutting wood for fuel and charcoal puts real pressure on forest resources: More than one-third of Jamaica's households rely on wood and charcoal for cooking and heating.

INDUSTRIES

Jamaica's manufacturing industry produces a wide range of goods and is a large employer. This sector is also an important source of export earnings. There are several types of industries including extractive industries, which yield products such as gypsum and cement; assembly industries, which produce items such as refrigerators and television sets; food processing, such as canned ackee and callaloo, milk, jam, and ice cream; chemical industries, such as converting sugar into rum, and bauxite into alumina; and the garment industry, in which garments are sewn for export. The garment industry uses imported cloth, which is sewn by Jamaican workers. Most manufacturing plants are located in the KMA, where there is a large labor supply and a developed transportation network.

Jamaica's economy is one of the most diversified in the Caribbean region. Growth in the manufacturing sector is especially encouraging. Much of Jamaican manufacturing is for local consumption, although Jamaican goods are shipped to neighboring Caribbean countries as well as to the United States, Canada, and Great Britain.

7

Living in Jamaica Today

J amaicans are modern people, and their life is not that different from that in the United States. They dress much like Americans, wearing Nikes, T-shirts, and jeans; watch television; listen to music; and go to movies. British influence is evident in sports and education. Today, popular culture, although uniquely Jamaican, is more often developed on the American model. Jamaica is not by any standard a rich country, and quality of life is low for many of the country's people.

FAMILY LIFE

Family life is central to most Jamaicans, although formal marriage is less common than in many other countries. Three generations may share a house. Many women have jobs, particularly in households in which men are absent; grandmothers normally take charge of preschool children. Wealthy Jamaicans employ domestic help.

None of the other reggae artists of the 1960s and 1970s achieved the fame of Bob Marley. Marley's music spoke to the daily struggles of Jamaicans in songs of faith, devotion, and revolution. He was a devout Rastafarian. This performance, in December 1976, was only 3 days after an assassination attempt that left him with gunshots in his left arm. Marley died of cancer at the age of 36.

MUSIC TODAY

Cricket, fast food, and Hollywood action movies are imported traits of Jamaica's contemporary popular culture. The country, however, has given birth to many homegrown expressions of pop culture.

In fact, Jamaican music, in particular, has become popular throughout much of the world. Jamaica's popular music has achieved widespread fame mainly through the emergence and spread of reggae. Reggae evolved from traditional Jamaican musical forms called mento (popular before the 1940s), ska (music of the 1950s), and rocksteady (named for its slow, steady beat). It was influenced by popular music developments in the United States, such as rock and roll and rhythm and blues.

Many reggae artists of the late 1960s and 1970s earned international fame for their original compositions, recordings, and performances. The best known of the island's artists was the late Bob Marley. He and his group, the Wailers, more than any other artist, was responsible for the "export" of reggae and its worldwide popularity. In recognition of his cultural contributions, Marley received Jamaica's Order of Merit, one of the country's highest national honors. He also was inducted into the American Rock and Roll Hall of Fame. Other reggae greats include Jimmy Cliff, Peter Tosh, Toots Hibbert, Jacob Miller, and Bunny Wailer. Recent Grammy Award winners in the reggae category include Jamaican artists such as the Melody Makers, Black Uhuru, Shabba Ranks, and Shaggy "Mr. Boombastic."

Jamaican popular music has continued to evolve. Dancehall, a type of postreggae music, has become the leading sound in Jamaican clubs and a major pop music export. In the late 1980s, "dancehall" became the new craze, complete with its own fashions of hairstyles and dress. Dancehall combines elements of reggae, disco, and rap. Soca (social calypso) is a mixture of American soul and calypso. It is especially popular during Carnival, a large springtime festival involving parades, costumes, and parties.

SPORTS AND RECREATION

Cricket and football (soccer) are the most popular sports in Jamaica. The British introduced cricket to Jamaica during the nineteenth century. The sport grew quickly in popularity. A number of West Indies cricket team captains have come from Jamaica.

In 1998, Jamaica's national soccer team, the Reggae Boyz, became the first team from the English-speaking Caribbean to qualify for World Cup finals. Jamaican athletes have excelled at track and field in Olympic competition, winning many medals. The country's women's netball and field hockey teams consistently have ranked among the world's best. In 1988, Jamaica even sent a bobsled team to the Calgary Winter Olympics! This team is the subject of the Walt Disney movie, *Cool Runnings*.

Recreation comes in many forms, from a day at the beach to an afternoon at a cricket match to an evening at the church or community center. A short list of recreational activities includes table tennis, field hockey, tennis, boxing, track and field, hiking, swimming, sailing, diving, and windsurfing. Horse racing is also popular. Dominoes are a favorite indoor game, played in rum bars and cafes. Music is everywhere. Leisure hours are often spent listening outside of rum bars to music coming from stereo systems. Young Jamaicans especially love to dance, and there are many discos, community centers, and clubs. Jamaicans also enjoy watching television and videos, listening to sports broadcasts, and going to movies. Children enjoy playing electronic games and basketball, which has become increasingly popular.

FESTIVALS AND PUBLIC HOLIDAYS

Jamaicans observe ten public holidays each year. They are New Year's Day, Ash Wednesday, Good Friday, Easter Monday, Labor Day, Emancipation Day, Independence Day, Heroes Day, Christmas, and Boxing Day.

Labour Day (May 23) originally celebrated the trade union movement. Since 1972, it has been a day for community service. Jamaicans join together in repairing roads, painting schools, planting trees and decorative shrubbery, and other tasks. Independence Day (the first Monday in August) is entirely given over to celebrations marking Jamaica's independence from Britain. National Heroes Day (Queen's birthday), the third Monday in October, recognizes the people who have made an impact on

Dancers perform a traditional folk dance during the National Independence Day parade in Kingston on August 6, 2003. This parade celebrated the country's forty-first anniversary of independence from Great Britain.

Jamaica. For most Jamaicans, Christmas is the biggest family event of the year. The day is celebrated by attending church services, exchanging gifts with family members, and gathering for a large meal. During the week between Christmas and New Year's, Jamaicans enjoy visiting the homes of friends and relatives.

Other than religious and national holidays, Jamaicans have a number of historic and cultural celebrations. On January 6, the Maroons (offsprings of escaped slaves) gather to celebrate the Accompong Maroon Festival. This event honors Kojo, who led the Maroons to a temporary victory over the British during the war of 1729 to 1739.

Throughout the Caribbean (and elsewhere), February is carnival month. In Kingston, the University of the West Indies hosts a two-week celebration each year. Events include calypso competitions, fashion shows, and all-night dances. Each spring, the country holds its own Jamaica Carnival, which begins on Easter and lasts for a week. Carnival is a combination of pageantry, spectacle, revelry, and calypso type (soca) music. In August, Jamaica Festival coincides with celebrations of Emancipation Day and Independence Day. The festival features competitions in all the major arts, as well as food preparation. People also enjoy beach parties and calypso, reggae, and soca music.

Several different ethnic groups hold their own celebrations. Some events include the Chinese New Year, the Hindu Diwali festival, and the Muslim observance of Hosay.

MODERN LITERATURE

Jamaican literature includes a diverse variety of folklore, essays, short stories, novels, and poetry. Much of the island's literary tradition developed following independence in 1962. A literary festival is held annually and includes competitions in writing poetry, short stories, and essays. Numerous Jamaican writers have received international awards in recognition of their work. They include Velma Pollard, author of *Karl and Other Stories* (1993), and the poet Kwame Dawes, author of *Progeny of Air* (1994). In the 1970s, a new art form called "dub poetry" emerged. In this genre, poems are often set to heavy reggae bass and drums.

JAMAICAN ART

The Jamaican art movement started in the 1920s and 1930s. It developed in close association with the Jamaican nationalist anticolonial movement. West African cultural traditions, which came along with the slave population, were actively repressed during the plantation period and its aftermath. In consequence, modern Jamaican art did not develop out of a continuous cultural tradition; instead, it evolved out of the conscious decision of a few pioneer artists, such as sculptress Edna Manley, to reject imposed colonial cultural identity. Although Jamaican art has changed tremendously since those pioneer days, this concern is still central to the work of contemporary Jamaican artists. The most common themes in Jamaica art are slavery, black consciousness, spirituality, the family, and nationalism. Other artists and art forms range from a tradition of wood carvers who sell their folk art wares along the highways, to internationally known sculptors and painters.

THEATER AND DANCE

Jamaica has lively theater and dance, mostly with a local flavor. Most theater is in Kingston. Plays often incorporate dance and include a message, sometimes concentrating on the plight of the poor or commentary on the slave era. Many performances, whether comedy, tragedy, or political satire, are bawdy, upbeat affairs. Most of the plays feature Jamaican patois. Jamaican pantomime is a distinctive art form completely different from British pantomime. Folklore is prominent and there is often audience participation. It is also characterized by song, dance, and satirical jabs at the political scene.

Jamaican dance covers classical, African, and contemporary forms. The acclaimed National Dance Theatre Company is based out of Kingston's Little Theater. The troupe, founded in 1962, is famed for its elaborate, colorful costumes and African themes.

COMMUNICATIONS

The word, whether written, spoken, or sung, is an integral part of Jamaican self-expression and creativity. The island's media befits a nation twice its size: There are three major daily newspapers, a dozen radio stations, and three national television stations. American television is received by a multitude of satellite dishes. Jamaica's extensive radio network broadcasts the news but most of all spreads Jamaican musical sounds throughout the island. Just as in the United States, cell phones abound.

LIVING STANDARDS

How high is the standard of living in Jamaica? Many Jamaicans do not think of Jamaica as a poor country, citing abundant natural resources and high literacy rates. Other Jamaicans see the high unemployment rate, lack of economic opportunity, poorly maintained roads, and deteriorating housing as clear signs of poverty. Whatever the opinion, Jamaica scores well in some categories of standard of living indicators. By certain other measures it fares badly. Favorable indicators are high adult literacy, age structure of the population, life expectancy at birth, and availability of electricity, water, and sewage disposal. A high crime rate, widespread poverty, and chronic unemployment are the downside.

Literacy

Literacy in Jamaica is high, 85 percent for the total population (89.1 percent for females and 80.8 percent rate for males).

Age Structure

Age structure pyramids give a lot of information about population growth, wealth, and health of countries. Poor countries will often have large numbers of children compared to numbers of working-age adults and older people. It is said that a country cannot develop until it has effectively controlled its population growth. This is seen in the age structure groupings with a decrease in size of the dependent population.

For Jamaica, the age groupings for 2003 are estimated to be

0–14 years: 28.6 percent (395,074 male; 376,870 female)

15–64 years: 64.5 percent (870,486 male; 869,431 female)

65 years and older: 6.8 percent (82,022 male; 101,984 female)

In the 0–14 years category, Jamaica stands at 117 of 223 nations in world, which is excellent for a developing country. This ranking is evidence of the success of an energetic program of family planning in effect since the early 1970s.

Health

Life expectancy at birth for the total population in Jamaica (2003 estimate) is 76 (74 years for males and 78 years for females). This ranks Jamaica sixty-third among 223 countries in the world, a relatively high rating. Troublesome diseases include cancer, stroke, diabetes, and HIV/AIDS. Homicide is the fifth leading cause of death in Jamaica, after disease.

Violence

Jamaica's murder rate of just over 40 per 100,000 (2002) ranks among the world's highest. Much of the violence is attributed to inner-city gangs linked to drug and gun trafficking. The remainder falls into the categories of domestic murder, revenge killing, and politically motivated clashes. A disproportionately high percentage of murders (67 percent of homicides) took place in the Kingston/St. Andrew Metropolitan Area and in St. Catherine. Combined, these two arenas account for less than 40 percent of the country's 2.6 million people. Jamaica's urban violence strikes fear in the people, is a drag on the economy, and threatens the tourist industry, especially in and around Kingston.

Poverty and Unemployment

Jamaica has two societies, one rich and the other quite poor. In 2002, it was estimated that approximately one-third of all Jamaicans had incomes below the poverty line. (Consumption is used as a proxy for income, because of the difficulties associated with getting reliable income information.) The incidence of poverty on the island continues to be highest in rural Jamaica. The wealthiest 20 percent of the population accounts for about 46 percent of national consumption, whereas the poorest 20 percent of the population accounts for only about 6 percent of all consumed goods and services. A chronically high unemployment rate, averaging around 15 percent (and an even greater rate of underemployment), continues to plague many island families. Such conditions are an expression of a depressed economy.

Electricity, Water, and Sewage

Jamaica is almost entirely electrified. Even most rural homes have power. About 84 percent of all Jamaicans have access to a reliable supply of clean water. Sewage systems are less well developed. The parishes with large urban centers, including Kingston/St. Andrew, St. Catherine (Portmore and Spanish Town), and St. James (Montego Bay) have generally better services than smaller towns and rural areas. In St. Andrew, approximately 70 percent of households have a piped water supply, whereas 40 percent of households lack their own sanitary facilities. In Kingston, however, approximately half of households lack piped water and 60 percent lack their own sanitary facilities. This is an extremely high figure for the country's major urban center.

A PERSPECTIVE ON QUALITY OF LIFE

Measured by U.S. standards, most Jamaicans suffer from extensive poverty, and the country itself is classified as being "less developed." Even within the Caribbean region, the country ranks next to last in terms of per capita gross national income, or purchasing power parity. Only Haiti is poorer. Does poverty always translate into a poor quality of life? Not necessarily. Many Jamaicans consider themselves well off when family and friends and the ability to provide the necessities of daily life are the measures of life quality.

One problem common to the Caribbean region is its close proximity to the affluent United States and Canada. This juxtaposition of poverty and wealth magnifies the statistical data and makes life more difficult for people who are able to see, envy, and want what their neighbors have. Nonetheless, most Jamaicans remain upbeat and optimistic about the future of their tropical land.

CHAPTER

8

Jamaica Looks to the Future

As a young nation, Jamaica has experienced a fair measure of inconsistency in its economic and political management. The country faces several major challenges to further development. A stagnating economy, currently beset by a variety of financial crises, must be jump-started. The island's fragile, but economically critical natural resource base must be protected. Prospects for an entire generation of Jamaican youth are at risk because of joblessness, poverty, crime, and violence. These conditions must be improved.

At independence, Jamaica was the gem of the Caribbean. The island country was experiencing considerable economic prosperity and its residents were enjoying one of the highest standards of living in the Caribbean region. Over the past decade, however, Jamaica's economic growth rate has become the second-lowest in the region, trailed only by impoverished Haiti. There are a number of reasons

Jamaican's children and future generations would benefit from programs to improve primary education. The students in low-income communities must be taught skills that will enhance their lives.

for the depressed economy. It is caused in part by declining prices for bauxite, sugar, and other commodities. There has also been a collapse of the financial sector, accompanied by low productivity and poor economic management. Jamaica needs to achieve broad-based economic growth by fostering competition, improving business skills, and investing in new businesses. Manufacturing has a bright future. Unlike other Caribbean islands, Jamaica can largely feed itself as long as its agricultural population is properly organized and encouraged.

Tourism in particular must be revived. The industry's infrastructure—hotels and restaurants, well-trained staff, transportation facilities and routes, and other things that tourists take for granted—is in place. Many potential tourists, however, are reluctant to travel to a land, even a tropical paradise, that is beset by high crime, drugs, and other social problems. If Jamaica is to succeed, it is imperative that tourism thrive. It provides the most obvious and certain key to the country's future economic development.

Jamaica's economy has long depended on tourism, mining, and agriculture (both traditional and plantation). These activities, however, have contributed to widespread degradation of the country's natural environment and resource base. Such conditions threaten the very existence of these key industries. Concentration of both population and economic activity in urban and coastal areas threatens natural habitats in these critically important areas. In response to these threats, both the Jamaican government and local nongovernmental organizations must direct efforts toward better managing and protecting Jamaica's fragile land and sea environments and resources.

Primary-level education needs to be improved. Particular emphasis must be given to educational programs in low-income communities, where youngsters must be taught skills that can enhance their lives. This is particularly important given the growing number of youth at risk, including those not in school.

CURBING CRIME

Crime, and especially violent crime, is rampant. Jamaica must find a way to protect its population. The core contributors to the problem, including unemployment, lack of economic opportunity, low wages, drugs, and drug trafficking, must be addressed aggressively.

POLITICAL FUTURE

The People's National Party (PNP) will hold political office until 2007. Given its narrow victory in the 2002 election, it may well be unseated by its rival, the Jamaica Labour Party, in the next national election. A change in Jamaica's constitution may be on the horizon. PNP leader Percival J. Patterson wants Jamaica to become a republic by the time he leaves office. Jamaica declared independence from Great Britain in 1962, but like 11 other Caribbean countries, it retains the queen as a ceremonial head of state. The main parties on the island are in favor, but they differ over the role of a new head of state. Patterson's governing PNP prefers an executive president elected by the people, whereas the JLP favors a largely ceremonial post.

In looking ahead, it is difficult to forecast the island country's future with any degree of certainty. In the introduction to this book, many of Jamaica's assets were spotlighted. They include the sea, a warm tropical climate and ecosystem, spectacular scenery, and close proximity to the United States and Canada. It has a fascinating, if occasionally turbulent, history and offers a rich, multicultural heritage and way of life. Most of its people are educated, and unlike many developing countries, Jamaica is not beset by problems of overpopulation. By nearly any measure, the country should be successful.

Contemporary problems already have been highlighted. If the country is to succeed, they must be conquered, and soon. Political responsibility, economic development, and social stability are tightly intertwined. If this is achieved, Jamaica is certain to once again achieve the status of "Gem of the Caribbean."

Fact at a Glance

Country Name	Jamaica
Location	In the Caribbean Sea, south of Cuba
Capital	Kingston
Area	4,244 total square miles (10,991 square kilometers); land area, 4,182 square miles (10,831 square kilometers), and water area, 62 square miles (160 square kilometers)
Land Features	Mountainous, with narrow, discontinuous coastal plain; highest point, Blue Mountain Peak, 7,204 feet (2,256 meters) in eastern Jamaica.
Climate	Tropical; hot, humid with temperate interior. High rainfall on the north and east side of island, drier on the south coast.
Major Water Features	120 rivers including Great River, Yallahs River, Black River, numerous springs
Natural Hazards	Hurricanes, earthquakes, landslides
Land Use	Arable land: 16.07% Permanent crops: 9.23% Other: 74.7% (1998 estimate)
Environmental Issues	Heavy rates of deforestation; coastal waters polluted by industrial waste, sewage, and oil spills; damage to coral reefs; air pollution in Kingston results from vehicle emissions
Population	2,695,867 (2003 estimate)
Population Growth Rate	0.61% (2003 estimate)
Total Fertility Rate	2.01, average number of children born to each woman during childbearing years (2003 estimate)
Life Expectancy at Birth	76 years (male, 74; female, 78; 2003 estimate)
Ethnic Groups	African, 91%; East Indian, 1%; European, 0.2%; Chinese, 0.2%; mixed ethnicity, 7%; other ethnic groups, 0.1%
Religion	Protestant, 61% (Church of God, 21%; Baptist, 9%; Anglican, 5%; Seventh-Day Adventist, 9%; Pentecostal, 8%; Methodist, 3%; United Church, 3%; Brethren, 1%; Jehovah's Witness, 1%; Moravian, 1%); Roman Catholic, 4%; other, including some spiritual cults 35%

Languages	English, Jamaican creole (patois)
Literacy	Total population: 88%; Male: 84%; Female: 92% (2003 estimate)
Type of Government	Constitutional parliamentary democracy
Executive Branch	Chief of state: English monarch, represented by the governor general
Head of government	Prime minister (after legislative elections, the leader of the majority party or the leader of the majority coalition in the House of Representatives is appointed prime minister by the governor general)
Independence	August 6, 1962 (from the United Kingdom)
Administrative Divisions	3 counties and 14 parishes
Currency	Jamaican dollar
Labor Force by Occupation	Services, 60%; Agriculture, 21%; Industry, 19%
Industries	Tourism, bauxite, textiles, food processing, light manufacturing, rum, cement, metal, paper, chemical products
Primary Exports	Alumina, bauxite, sugar, bananas, rum
Export Partners	($1.4 billion, 2002 estimate) United States, 36%; Europe (excluding the United Kingdom), 16%; United Kingdom, 13%; Canada, 11%
Imports	($3 billion, 2002 estimate) Machinery and transport equipment, construction materials, fuel, food, chemicals, fertilizers
Import Partners	United States, 48%; CARICOM countries (14 Caribbean countries), 12%; Europe, 8%; Latin America, 7%
Transportation	Highways (total): 11,806 miles (19,000 kilometers). Paved: 8,347 miles (13,433 kilometers). Railroads: 169 miles (272 kilometers); 129 miles (207 kilometers), belonging to the Jamaica Railway Corporation, no longer operational; the remaining track is privately owned and used to transport bauxite. Airports: 35 (11 paved). Ports and Harbors: Alligator Pond, Discovery Bay, Kingston, Montego Bay, Ocho Rios, Port Antonio, Rocky Point, Port Esquivel (Longswharf)

Primary source: 2003 *CIA World Factbook, Jamaica*

650	Taino Indians from Guyana and Venezuela come to Jamaica.
1494	Christopher Columbus lands at St. Ann's Bay.
1510	Spanish colonists arrive, establishing Sevilla la Nueva on St. Ann's Bay (north coast) and Spanish Town (Villa de la Vega) on the south coast.
1517	The first African slaves are imported to replace native peoples as labor.
1655	The British capture Jamaica from Spanish.
1662	The population is 3,653 whites, 552 slaves, total 4,205.
1663	Jews start settling in Jamaica.
1664	Four hundred planters come from Barbados.
1670	Spain cedes Jamaica to the British by the Treaty of Madrid. There are 70 sugar works in Jamaica.
1673	The population is 7,768 whites, 9,504 slaves, total 17,272.
1675	One thousand one hundred Surinam settlers arrive in St. Elizabeth.
1690	Slaves rebel in Clarendon and escape to join the Maroons. The First Maroon War begins.
1692	A violent earthquake destroys Port Royal.
1693	Kingston is laid out.
1728	Sir Nicholas Lawes introduces coffee to Jamaica from the French West Indies.
1739	A peace treaty is concluded between the British and the Maroons, ending the First Maroon War. Peace lasts for the next 50 years. There are 429 sugar works in Jamaica.
1744	Earthquake and hurricane destroy Savanna-la-Mar and badly damage Kingston and Port Royal.
1760	Slaves rebel in Port Maria under Tackey's leadership; 60 whites and 400 slaves are killed.
1764	The population reaches 166,454 (146,454 slaves).

1768	There are 651 sugar works in Jamaica.
1775	The population reaches 209,617 (12,737 whites, 4,093 free colored, 192,787 slaves).
1777	A slave rebellion is followed by 30 executions.
1780–1781	Savanna-La-Mar is destroyed, Westmoreland is devastated, and 120 vessels in Kingston Harbor are wrecked by hurricanes.
1782	Slaves rebel in St. Mary's under Three-Fingered Jack's leadership.
1785	The population includes 30,000 whites, 10,000 free colored, 250,000 slaves.
1793	Breadfruit is brought from Tahiti to Jamaica.
1796	The Second Maroon War begins. Dogs are brought in to hunt Maroons in the Cockpit Country; 600 Maroons are deported to Nova Scotia and later moved to Sierra Leone.
1807	The Slave trade is abolished. The population reaches 319,351.
1831	A slave uprising in St. James, Trelawney, Hanover, Westmoreland, St. Elizabeth, and Manchester is sparked by Sam Sharpe; 200 are killed in the field and about 500 are executed.
1834	Slavery is abolished and the apprenticeship system is established.
1838	Slavery is officially ended.
1844	The population reaches 377,433.
1845	The Jamaica Railway is established.
1850	An Asiatic cholera epidemic breaks out; 32,000 die.
1854	Four hundred seventy-two Chinese come to Jamaica from Panama.
1865	The rebellion at Morant Bay occurs.
1871	The population reaches 506,154.
1872	The capital is moved from Spanish Town to Kingston.
1907	An earthquake, followed by several major fires, destroys most of Kingston - Port Royal. Kingston is rebuilt.

History at a Glance

1938 Violence and rioting take place on several sugar plantations. Alexander Bustamante forms the Bustamante Industrial Trade Union and the Jamaica Labour Party. Norman Manley establishes the socialist People's National Party.

1942 Bauxite is discovered in St. Ann's Parish and subsequently in many areas of the island.

1944 The Constitution, based on universal adult suffrage, is put in place and ends the Crown Colony period.

1951 Hurricane Charlie badly damages Kingston, Port Royal, and Morant Bay.

1957 An earthquake measuring 8 on the Richter Scale shakes Jamaica. The epicenter is Hanover in St. James Parish.

1962 Jamaica achieves in independence from British rule. Bustamante is the country's first prime minister. He is succeeded by Donald Sangster, who serves only a few months in office. Hugh Shearer replaces Sangster.

1963 Hurricane Flora strikes Jamaica.

1966 Haile Selassie, emperor of Ethiopia, King of Kings, Conquering Lion of Judah, arrives on three-day state visit. He addresses parliament and receives an honorary doctorate.

1969 Norman Washington Manley dies. The holiday for the queen's birthday is discontinued, and National Heroes Day is established on October 20, 1969, to be celebrated on the third Monday in October each year thereafter.

1972 Michael Manley, son of Norman Manley, heads a socialist government. He forges links with Cuba over the objections of the United States. The economy begins to decline and country goes through a period of unrest.

1973 Jamaica helps found the Caribbean Community and Common Market (CARICOM), together with the Barbados, Guyana, and Trinidad and Tobago.

1977 Sir Alexander Bustamante dies at the age of 94. He is the last surviving National Hero of Jamaica.

1980	A new government, led by Edward Seaga, is formed. It has strong support from the United States. Tourism recovers and expands.
1981	Jamaica and the world mourn the death of Bob Marley, reggae superstar.
1988	Hurricane Gilbert hits the island with winds of 120 miles per hour; 80 percent of houses on the south coast of the island are damaged or destroyed.
1989	Michael Manley and the PNP win the general elections and return to office.
1992	Michael Manley, prime minister and leader of the People's National Party (PNP) for 23 years, leaves office because of ill health and is succeeded by Percival J. Patterson.
1993	Prime Minister Patterson and the PNP win general elections, and the JLP announces that it will boycott the parliament in protest of the "fraudulent" election conduct and the "partisan" role of the police.
1997	Michael Manley dies.
1999	The country erupts in riots after the government announced a 30 percent increase in the tax on gasoline. Kingston and Montego Bay, where sugar cane fields were set ablaze, are particularly badly hit. After three days of arson and looting, the tax is rescinded.

Further Reading

Banks, Russell. *The Book of Jamaica.* Harpercollins, 1996.

Barrett, Leonard E. *The Rastafarians,* Beacon Press, 1997.

Benghiat, Norma. *Traditional Jamaican Cookery.* Penguin Books,1985.

Cliff, Michelle. *Abeng.* Penguin, 1985.

Dunn-Smith, Paulette and Wintlett Browne. *Jamaica: Living Together in Society.* Carlong Publishers, 1998.

Gotlieb, Karla. *The Mother of Us All: A History of Queen Nanny, Leader of the Windward Maroons.* Africa World Press, 2000.

Go-Local Jamaica.
http://www.go-kingston.com

Jamaica Gleaner.
http://jamaica-gleaner.com

Kurlansky, Mark. A *Continent of Islands.* Perseus Books,1992.

Lewis, Mathew. *Journal of a West India Proprietor Kept during a Residence in the Island of Jamaica.* Edited by Judith Terry. Oxford World's Classics, 1999

Lucie-Smith, Edward. *Albert Huile–Father of Jamaican Painting.* Kingston. Ian Randle Publishers, 2001.

Morris, Pam, Sonia Glanville, and Wintlette Browne. *Jamaica: Living Together in Society.* Carlong Publishers, 2000.

O'Sullivan-Sirjue, Jennifer, Eleanor Jones, Darcy Wright, and Elizabeth Stevens. *Jamaica: Land and People.* Carlong Publishers, 1998.

Pawson, Michael and David Buisseret. *Port Royal Jamaica.* Norman: University of Oklahoma, 2000 (1975).

Sherlock, Philip and Hazel Bennet. *The Story of Jamaican People.* Markus Wiener, 1997.

Tanna, Laura. *Jamaican Folk Tales and Oral Histories.* Kingston: Institute of Jamaica Publications, 1993.

White, Timothy. *Catch a Fire: The Life of Bob Marley.* Guernsey Press,1983.

Winkler, Anthony C. *Going Home to Teach.* LMH Publishing, 1995.

Index

Index

Index

Index

page:

9:	New Millennium Images	49:	© CORBIS
10:	© Lucidity Information Design, LLC	53:	© Howard Davies/CORBIS
15:	© Lucidity Information Design, LLC	58:	21st Century Publishing
18:	New Millennium Images	60:	AFP/NMI
21:	New Millennium Images	65:	© Howard Davies/CORBIS
29:	AP/Wide World Photos	71:	KRT/NMI
32:	AP/Wide World Photos	79:	AP/Wide World Photos
34:	New Millennium Images	83:	KRT/NMI
38:	© Bettmann/CORBIS	87:	AP/Wide World Photos
43:	KRT/NMI	90:	AP/Wide World Photos
44:	KRT/NMI	97:	KRT/NMI
47:	AP/Wide World Photos		

Cover: © Howard Davies/CORBIS

About the Contributors

JANET H. GRITZNER is a Professor of Geography at South Dakota State University at Brookings. She started her career as a cultural geographer, but now teaches courses in Geographic Information Systems (GIS). She has worked and traveled in a number of countries in Africa (e.g., Senegal, Gambia, Botswana, Kenya) and the Caribbean (e.g., Jamaica, Antigua, Bahamas, Guadeloupe, Puerto Rico). She has had a lifelong interest in studying Caribbean food ways. She has spoken to many audiences about the culture history of Jamaica food habits and is in the process of writing a book on the range and diversity of diet in the Caribbean. This fascinating topic is as much as anything an excuse to sample the many delicious foods eaten by people throughout the Caribbean region. She has no objection, however, of trying new foods wherever she travels in the world.

CHARLES F. ("FRITZ") GRITZNER is Distinguished Professor of Geography at South Dakota University in Brookings. He is now in his fifth decade of college teaching and research. During his career, he has taught more than 60 different courses, spanning the fields of physical, cultural, and regional geography. In addition to his teaching, he enjoys writing, working with teachers, and sharing his love for geography with students. As consulting editor for the MODERN WORLD NATIONS series, he has a wonderful opportunity to combine each of these "hobbies." Fritz has served as both President and Executive Director of the National Council for Geographic Education and has received the Council's highest honor, the George J. Miller Award for Distinguished Service.